Starting & Running Your Own Horse Business

Second Edition

STARTING & RUNNING YOUR OWN HORSE BUSINESS

BY MARY ASHBY McDONALD, DVM

Storey Publishing

The mission of Storey Publishing is to serve our customers by publishing practical information that encourages personal independence in harmony with the environment.

Edited by Deborah Burns
Art direction and book design by Mary Winkelman Velgos
Text production by Liseann Karandisecky

Front cover photograph by © 2009 Mark J. Barrett, www.markjbarrett.com
Author photo by Dr. William Janecke, Christian Veterinary Mission, Santa Cruz, Bolivia
Interior photography by © Dusty Perin/www.dustyperin.com, except for page 9, Dr. William Janecke, Christian Veterinary Mission, Santa Cruz, Bolivia
Illustrations by Jim Dyekman, 84 and 85; Joanna Rissanen, 86; and © Elayne Sears, 171
Horseshoe icon by © iStockphoto.com

Indexed by Samantha Miller/Sciendex

Storey Publishing
210 MASS MoCA Way
North Adams, MA 01247
www.storey.com

Printed in the United States by Malloy Incorporated
10 9 8 7 6 5 4 3 2 1

Library of Congress Cataloging-in-Publication Data
McDonald, Mary Ashby, 1959–
Starting & running your own horse business / Mary Ashby McDonald. — 2nd ed.
p. cm.
Includes index.
ISBN 978-1-60342-483-7 (pbk. : alk. paper)
1. Horse industry. 2. Horse farms—Management. 3. Stables—Management.
4. New business enterprises. 5. Small business—Management. I. Title.
II. Title: Starting and running your own horse business. III. Title: Horse business.
HD9434.A2.M33 2009
636.10068—dc22

2009023771

CONTENTS

I dedicate this book to my husband, Jack McDonald III,
and to my children, Ashby and Jack IV.
Thanks for believing in me, loving me, and persevering with me.

*"Some trust in chariots and some in horses,
but we trust in the name of the Lord our God."*
Psalm 20:7

Acknowledgments

I would like to thank the following people: Mr. and Mrs. M. Pierce Ashby, for purchasing my first pony, Duke, and enabling me to earn a bachelor's degree in animal science from Virginia Polytechnic Institute and State University; Catherine Ashby Akins, for her invaluable contributions and support; Charlie D. Akins, for taking me to my first horse show; Pat Betts, for giving me my first riding lessons and teaching me and hundreds of others how to ride properly; Susan DeBries, English professor, Day Star University, Nairobi, Kenya; Joe Fargis, for teaching me how to "equitate" as a "junior," and, along with Conrad Homfeld, being my first employer in the horse business; Kathy Farrow; Sarah Fletcher, M.D.; and Dr. A.N. Huff.

"Building a User Base" is adapted from the article, "Horse Marketing: Expanding the User Base," May 1988, written by Dr. A.N. Huff, Extension animal scientist emeritus, and is used with his permission. Sections on breeding are adapted from *The Selection and Promotion of the Breeding Stallion*, by Steve G. Jennings. This excellent self-published book is available through S.J. Publications, P.O. Box 615, Front Royal, VA 22630.

I would also like to thank Betty, Mike, and Tim Jennings, of Professional Auction Services, Inc.; Maribel Koella, a partner with Collins, Sharp & Koella; Melissa Aberle Johnson; Pam Marks, Marks Insurance and Associates, Inc., Germantown, Maryland; Dr. Thomas N. Meacham; Jack McDonald III, Chartered Financial Analyst; Trish Palys, equestrian trainer; Barbara Person, equine insurance specialist; Susan Smith; Daniel W. Sutherland and Elise J. Sutherland; Susan Terranella, manager, Rio Vista Farm, Leander, Texas; Carla McDonald Hawkinson, President, Board of Directors, Tennessee Valley Hunt; Dea Kelly Thomas, Master of Foxhounds, Tennessee Valley Hunt; Alexandra W. Malik, owner of Medway Ranch, for having faith in me and giving me the opportunity to manage her ranch; Dr. Nathaniel White, Marion Dupont Equine Medical Center, Leesburg, Virginia; and Teri Abrams, Harmony Hills Equestrian Center.

PREFACE

This book is designed for anyone interested in reducing expenses and making money in the horse business. Some people will say this is an unrealistic notion, but it really *is* possible to keep costs down and maintain a positive cash flow.

In 1982, I took over management of the Medway Ranch in Austin, Texas. The ranch was practically unknown to the public. There was no letterhead, logo, colors, brochures — not even an ad in the Yellow Pages. Through the application of sound business practices, including an advertising and promotion campaign, the ranch turned into a respected, profitable enterprise in just a few years.

By making a horse business successful, we reap more than just monetary reward. We can better appreciate the many pleasures that attracted us to horses in the first place. There is the gratification of walking into a clean barn, where well-kept horses are munching on sweet-smelling hay. Do you remember the first time one of your green horses accomplished a flying lead change? Or the delight in the eyes of a parent whose young son received his certificate for horsemanship at summer day camp? How about the students who come to you as beginners and ultimately win a handful of ribbons at a show, or the tremendous pride you feel when one of your horses or students progresses to the U.S. Equestrian Team? These are the joys that make laboring through the hot days of summer and frigid winter nights in the barn worth the effort — and make you grateful you don't have a desk job. Some of us believe it's the ultimate in mixing business with pleasure.

Whether you own or board one horse or 100, the goals of this book are to provide you with many ways to save money, labor, and time, and to make your job easier and more profitable. As you read, keep a list of the ideas that you would like to use in your own operation. Put an expected date of completion next to each entry on your list, then follow through.

Here's wishing you the best with your business.

— Mary Ashby McDonald, DVM

By making a horse business successful, we reap more than just monetary reward. We can better appreciate the many pleasures that attracted us to horses in the first place.

INTRODUCTION

WHY WOULD ANYONE GO INTO THE HORSE BUSINESS?

"This horse thing won't ever turn you loose."

— Helen Kitner Crabtree, legendary trainer, instructor, author, member of World Championship Horse Show Hall of Fame, and first woman to be named Horse Trainer of the Year

What is it about horses? What *is* this "horse thing that will never turn you loose"?

I believe it is a physical, emotional, and spiritual bond. In other words, it's love.

My first love was Duke, an 11.3-hand Shetland stud pony. My parents bought him for my tenth birthday, not knowing any better. The kids in my neighborhood had ponies the way most kids have bikes, and we galloped all over Powhatan

County, Virginia, like banshees on the warpath, bareback and barefoot, having the time of our lives. In the lazy summer afternoons I would take Duke down to graze on the banks of the James River while I sat on his back devouring all of the Marguerite Henry and Walter Farley books.

Duke taught me more than any riding instructor ever could. He comforted me through the tumultuous teen years, the death of my mother, and my difficult family life. Many nights I wept into his mane. Years later I went to see him on my wedding day to get a blessing, and still later I took my first-born daughter Ashby and sat her on his back. At that point he was ancient and nearly blind but still a perfect gentleman. A few years later (at 47 years old!) he died, and again I wept. I wept at the passing of my mentor, my hero, my soul friend; the connection to and solace of my past now gone.

Since then as an equine veterinarian I have had to euthanize many of my clients' old horses and to stand with them as they watched their soul companion breathe his last breath. There is a wrenching of the souls as they part. Many of you will get choked up reading this because you have experienced this same "horse thing." The emotional bond is undefinable, as pointed out by Beryl Markham, the first woman to receive her jockey's license in Kenya: "A lovely horse is always an experience . . . . It is an emotional experience of the kind that is spoiled by words."

So why would anyone go into the horse business? I asked my friend Dr. Julia McCann, Horse Science Specialist at Virginia Tech, and she replied, "I think the only reason you go into the horse business is because that is the only place you can imagine yourself being happy. With the right insight, knowledge base, work ethic, set of contacts, marketing skills, and a blessing from above, one *can* make money in the horse business, and make enough to pay for one's own 'habit'."

You must go into the horse business because you love it. You love it more than any other profession. It is long, hard work, and only gumption and love will get you through the long, hot summers and cold winters. Do not go into it for the large sums of money you hope to make!

Dr. Mary McDonald in Bolivia training village Animal Health Care Workers in how to do intravenous injections.

When the first edition of *Starting & Running Your Own Horse Business* came out, I autographed a book a father was buying for his daughter. He asked, "Do you know how to make a small fortune with horses?"

Excited, I asked, "No, how?'

He quipped, "Start with a large one!"

Living out our passions rarely has to do with making large sums of money; it has more to do with exercising our God-given gifts and fulfilling our dreams. I want to encourage you to "Do Your Dream." Fulfill your passion for going into the horse business, not just for yourself but for all the others for whom you will provide a "Duke experience." You can give others the gift of horseback riding, or employment in the field they love, or riding in a carriage to their wedding.

As you read through *Starting & Running Your Own Horse Business* you will find countless ways to do your dream from starting a lesson program and running camps to breeding horses and boarding. This edition includes a new chapter on starting and running a carriage business and, because I've become a veterinarian since I first published this book, another on how to save money on veterinary care. You will also see chapters on how to advertise and manage the business part of the operation including many money-making ideas such as buying and selling horses and opening your own tack shop.

My prayer is that my book will inspire you to fulfill your life calling and use your God-given gifts to do your dream — because "this horse thing won't ever turn you loose."

PART I

Business 101

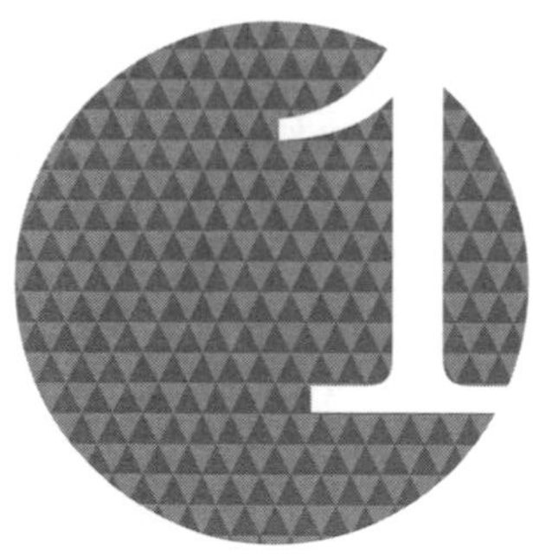

MANAGING YOUR BUSINESS

Most equestrians go into business because they know and love horses, not because they want to reconcile bank statements, organize files, or plan calendars. Successfully managing your records and finances, however, is instrumental in making a profit in this business.

I know how hard it is to become and stay organized when you have so many other things going on. Several times I have taken checks from students in the middle of lessons and stuffed them in my dusty pocket, only to recover crumbled, illegible bits of paper from my washing machine a week later.

Lack of organization results in lost opportunities, lost time, and lost dollars. It takes time, planning, and diligence to create and maintain organization, but you can simplify the process by following the advice in this section.

Time Management

The horse business is long, hard work. It often requires putting in 7-day weeks and, if you have a colicky horse or a foaling mare, 24-hour days. Don't work harder; work smarter. Start by carefully planning your time.

Begin each morning by planning what you want to accomplish that day. Make a "To Do" list and give each task a priority. If you have a list of 10 tasks that need to be accomplished, you may have two that are "A" priorities. Do those first. Don't fall victim to the "tyranny of the urgent."

Let's say you schedule an important staff meeting for noon and someone calls 15 minutes before the meeting and wants to come and look at a horse. Don't tell the potential customer to come at noon; have him come after the staff meeting. When possible, stick with your priorities.

Be sure to utilize idle time. For example, you can fit in phone calls or bookwork between classes at horse shows, or between customers while selling tack. (See chapter 10 for information on opening a tack shop.)

Need Help?

There are many good CDs on time management and business management available online and at your local library or bookstore. Listen to them while you are driving to the feed store or hauling horses.

Labor Management

Closely monitor the wages you pay for labor to make sure they don't exceed your budget. Careful planning can cut these costs dramatically. Install labor-saving devices, such as automatic horse waterers, which cost about $30 each, or float-operated waterers, which cost about $10 each. Remember, you are paying for labor every time a horse is watered. In some parts of the country, catfish are placed in outdoor water tubs to keep tubs clean, further saving on labor costs.

Consider this: If you have 60 horses in the barn:

- 3 hours/day are spent watering
- 3 hours × $7.25/hour wage = $21.75
- $21.75/day × 365 days a year = $7,938.75/year
- $7,938.75/year × 10 years = $79,387.50 spent in labor costs just for watering horses

The manager at Harmony Hills Equestrian Center, a successful riding and boarding enterprise, adds her perspective on labor savings.

Labor Management Cost-Savers

- **Establish cooperative programs with agricultural schools.** These programs often require a semester or more of work experience for students. You may provide room, board, or just a small stipend in exchange for their labor.
- **Establish work-study programs for junior and senior high-school students.** Allow them to exchange work for lessons, leasing, or board. Closely supervise these programs and make adjustments as necessary.
- **Set clear responsibilities and schedules** for all employees so you don't have to spend time checking up on jobs and reminding people what they have to do. Your employees can work much more efficiently if they know horses are fed at 7:00 A.M. and 5:00 P.M., that stalls are cleaned by 10:30 A.M., and that horses are brought in from the pastures by 3:30 P.M.
- **Practice good management;** it saves money as well as headaches. You can buy or borrow books, DVDs, and CDs on management that will give you other money-saving pointers.

"You can take on the chores all yourself, but may find as the years roll on this becomes harder and harder to do. Labor is expensive so you can cut costs by doing a volunteer program or work exchange. Have your helpers trade lessons or rides for barn chores. You need to take the time to supervise and train, and the turnover can be frustrating, but it is a cheap way to get help. Also look to the older, semiretired population, which is growing in our society. They will often work for less pay, but enjoy the job and can be a very stable, hard-working asset. Our full-time handyman is 63 and going strong!"

Make your own jumps and game equipment. This is not as hard as it may seem. There are a lot of books out there, and you can be creative! You can even make a work day out of it with your students and families for help.

If you live in areas that dip below freezing in winter, it may be a good investment to buy a floating deicer ($25), insulated bucket holder ($85), or a heated single-sided tank ($500). Do a cost analysis and see how much time is currently wasted by breaking the ice off the water buckets. Also factor in the possibility of a horse getting impaction colic from not wanting to drink the frigid water, and the veterinary bills that can result.

STAFF INPUT

Regularly hold staff brainstorming sessions. Your employees' input aids greatly in the planning process, and good communication is essential to being organized. Regular staff meetings not only keep everyone up to speed on barn business, they also give employees an opportunity to air grievances and contribute suggestions to resolve problems.

Make sure employees feel that they are heard. For example, if instructors tell you that the dust is so bad in the rings that they and riding students are choking on it, investigate the possibility of installing a sprinkler system or set up a regular sprinkler schedule during dry seasons.

Next, set a date for a planning retreat. The most productive sessions are held off grounds. Getting away will prevent distractions or interruptions from neighing horses, ringing phones, and talkative students. The getaway could be an

How to Conduct a Staff Meeting

Scheduling

1. Set date, time, location.
2. Notify staff.
3. Arrange for refreshments, equipment, and handouts.
4. Remind participants several days in advance.

Agenda

1. Determine topics to be covered and length of time required.
2. Prioritize agenda items.
3. Print agenda and make enough copies for handouts.

Meeting

1. Stick to the agenda.
2. Encourage full participation by calling on the quiet staff members, curtailing monopolization by a few, avoiding unnecessary rabbit trails, staying focused, and covering the agenda.
3. Have fun breaks, relax, laugh (humor defuses tension), treat your staff to good food, and reward them for all of the stalls they have mucked and frozen buckets they have broken.

Closing

1. Review plans.
2. Make sure everyone understands the assignments.
3. Schedule a meeting to see what changes have occurred.
4. Remind them, "If nothing changes, nothing changes."
5. Adjourn on time.

elaborate weekend at a bed-and-breakfast or a breakfast meeting at a local fast-food restaurant.

As you begin planning, focus first on the big picture to avoid getting bogged down in details. Set short-term (6-month) and long-term (1-year, 5-year, and 10-year) goals for your advertising, facilities, events/programs, horses, vehicles, and employees. Keep in mind that issues change, and these goals should be revisited and updated regularly.

Tech Tip

Search online to find free, printable weekly, monthly, and yearly calendars. These enable you to type in notes, appointments, and action points, and print out a customized calendar.

Organizational Planning

Don't let that old adage, "At the end of the day, when all is said and done, more is said than done!" be true of your operation. Planning ahead and organizing your business will help you achieve your goals. The following suggestions for organizing your calendars and "To Do" lists will get you started.

TIME ORGANIZATION: MASTER CALENDAR

Calendars are essential tools, and there are a variety of ways they can help keep you efficient and your business profitable.

365-Day Calendar

First you need a 12-month calendar to help you organize an overall plan of what you want accomplished throughout the year. I suggest the plastic "At A Glance" type that uses wet-erase markers. (Suggestion: Don't keep any permanent markers in your office if you are going to have these calendars. If, however, someone does write on this or a dry-erase board with a permanent marker you can write over it immediately with a wet-erase maker and it will wipe off.)

Taking the time to plan is the key to a successful business.

30-Day Calendar

Next, turn to the monthly calendar and write down what day you are going to do the specific task. For example, you might write for February 2: "Turn in soil sample for soil testing pastures and hay fields." Then, for February 25, soil test results now in hand, make a note to call the feed and seed store and get lime or fertilizer spread.

7-Day Calendar

Finally, on your weekly calendar, which you can keep with you in your PDA or Day-Timer, or pin on the wall, keep a daily "To Do" list with specific details. For example: "Farrier to do Sassy, Waffles & Katie, 12:00."

Other Ways to Use Your Calendar

- Advertising calendar: when and where to advertise and how much it will cost
- Budget
- Building and maintenance calendar: what needs to be built or repaired and when it should be done
- Event/program calendar: lessons, horse shows, clinics
- Training and sales calendar: the number of weeks each horse needs to reach his optimal condition and obtain the maximum sale price, when to enter each horse in a show where he will do his best and gain high visibility, and an estimated date by which horses should be sold
- Vehicle maintenance calendar: repairs, tune-ups, new tires, and so forth. It is essential to keep current maintenance records on vehicles. Once I was told the farm truck needed an entire new braking system. After checking the maintenance chart, I realized it had been done just 10 months earlier. I promptly took the truck to another mechanic, who agreed the brakes were fine. (See the Vehicles Maintenance Record in appendix H, page 203.)
- Vehicle replacement calendar: when to sell older vehicles (based on condition and depreciation) and buy new ones, and how much to save monthly to replace them
- Veterinary calendar: annual vaccinations, deworming, Coggins tests, floating teeth

Charting Your Course

Sit down and plan which month you want to do what activities and write the events on the calendar. Think through when your slow times are, when you can do some maintenance and overall planning, staff meetings, and so on. Map out busy times, summers, camps, tax time, and your and your staff's vacation time.

For example, during winter months you may plan pasture, barn, and fence maintenance; spring is vaccination time; summer is for shows; fall is for winterizing the place. Jot onto the yearly calendar the general task you plan to accomplish at the beginning of a week.

Show Your True Colors!

Paint your equipment with your farm colors to prevent others from mistaking it for their own and to keep equipment from getting lost or stolen at shows and events. Stencil your initials on buckets and tack boxes or wrap colored tape around the handles of pitchforks and brooms.

PHYSICAL ORGANIZATION

Here are some tips and tricks to keep you organized in space as well as in time.

- Post a list of contents on the inside doors of cabinets. This makes it easy to locate supplies and, if you note when an item is running low, you'll see at a glance when additional purchases need to be made. If you're using your medical supplies to treat your client's horses, be sure to charge the client for the product and the administration time. If you don't, you will end up running out of supplies and time without being reimbursed for either.
- Label exactly where equipment such as bridles and saddles should hang. To indicate where tools such as pitchforks and shovels go, outline their shapes on the wall with spray paint. This reminds workers and students to return them to their proper place, and helps you spot missing tools and borrowed stable equipment.
- Assign a tidy person to be in charge of keeping the tack room organized. Well-maintained tack is vital to the smooth operation of your farm. When tack is cleaned and properly stored, it lasts longer than if it is left scattered around the farm. Arrange the tack room so that visitors see the most organized section of the room; put dirty blankets or tack waiting to be cleaned in a less visible place.

A neatly organized tack room encourages students to keep tack clean and in place.

- Be creative when organizing equipment. I used to waste time searching for crops and lounge whips because there wasn't a designated place for them. I solved the problem by storing them in an umbrella canister.

OPERATIONAL ORGANIZATION

An organized office, using smart systems and procedures, will save you time and money in the long run.

- Computers — essential modern-day timesavers — are discussed on page 54. They are master organizers and timesavers, so if you don't have a computer now, seriously consider purchasing one. When talking to a salesperson, be clear about the computer's intended uses so you come home with the right computer and software to help run your business.
- Use bulletin boards and chalkboards to communicate with employees and clients. Post important emergency phone numbers on a bulletin board next to the phone, and special feeding requests on a chalkboard near the feed bin.
- Create files on students, boarders, business associates, suppliers, veterinarians, farriers, and so on. (See the appendixes for various forms you may want to keep on file.)
- Keep charts to help you and the staff track breeding, exercise, feeding, and shoeing schedules for your horses. (See Shoeing Record in appendix B, page 197.)
- Once a year, conduct a complete inventory of all equipment, facilities, tack, supplies, horses, employees, programs, and vehicles. Evaluate what should stay, what should go, what's missing, and what needs to be replaced.

PERSONNEL ORGANIZATION

Establish a schedule for meeting with each staff member privately and with the staff as a group. Discuss as appropriate:

- Employee reviews
- Hiring, firing, and training needs
- Instructor skill reviews
- Raises and promotions

Once you begin this process, you may recognize additional areas that could be organized more efficiently. Review the Organization Calendar in appendix J, page 209.

Office Supplies

Spend money on organizational products for the office. You may, however, be able to find many of the products you need at your local thrift store, like the Salvation Army or Goodwill. Another possibility is to visit a Habitat for Humanity's ReStore, where they sell everything from bookshelves to computer desks, and all of the proceeds go to a good cause.

Purchase other office organizers such as Rolodexes, business-card holders, organizational trays, and filing cabinets that will help you organize your business.

Loss of Use

Another type of horse insurance is for loss of use. The specifics will vary with the policy, but here's an example of how this coverage can work: You insure a valuable jumper under a policy that covers the horse specifically for this use. The horse then sustains a permanent injury. The insurer would pay the owner 60–75 percent of the insured amount and the horse would remain with the owner. Or the insurer would pay the owner 75 percent of the insured amount and potentially take possession of the horse.

Under such contracts, insurers have the right to have the horse destroyed but usually will try to sell the horse for some other use, perhaps as a companion or trail horse. To purchase loss-of-use coverage, you must purchase mortality and major medical coverage.

Good communication is essential for a well-run operation.

Insurance

Insurance is integral to good business planning. It's a necessary expense; without it, losses and liabilities could destroy everything you've worked to accomplish.

HEALTH INSURANCE

Providing health insurance to employees, even if you can afford to pay only a portion of the premium, is an excellent way to attract and retain good workers. Employees with access to health care are more likely to stay healthy, which means fewer lost days of work and a more productive performance at work.

If you decide to provide health insurance, shop among several insurers for the best premium on coverage that meets the needs of your employees. The least expensive insurance tends to be a group insurance policy with a high deductible. Ask whether the plan you are considering contracts with hospitals convenient to the farm, and whether most employees will be able to continue using their own physicians. Look online for tips for buying health insurance.

HORSE INSURANCE

Two primary types of insurance for horses are mortality insurance and major medical coverage. If you could not afford to replace a horse if something happened to him, mortality insurance is probably a good idea. When weighing this decision, be sure to ask specifically what causes of injury or death are included.

Policies for major medical coverage differ but, according to one equine insurance agent, coverage is usually limited to $7,500 to $10,000 per animal per year, and there is often a $250 deductible per incident or illness. Major medical would provide coverage for necessary surgical procedures, such as for colic. In addition, it would help cover expenses for other costly medical problems, such as Potomac Horse Fever, or a lameness problem such as Laminitis, once they exceed $250. To obtain major medical coverage, you may have to buy mortality coverage as part of the package.

There are some common restrictions on insurance policies covering horses. Many companies will not insure a horse over age 15 for major medical events, although it is possible to obtain mortality coverage for older horses. Coverage for preexisting conditions is also likely to be excluded. If a horse requiring colic surgery has to have an intestinal resection, you will find that most insurers will not insure that horse for colic in the future. If a horse has a bout with colic that requires only nonsurgical medical treatment, or undergoes colic surgery but does not require a resection, colic coverage will be removed from the policy; once the horse is colic free for one year, coverage for colic may again be restored.

Certainly, insuring horses against mortality and major medical bills is expensive, but it is a good investment if you have a major medical event. It is comforting to know you can cover the bill and provide the treatment. Insurance is not always worth the money, however, such as if you have 10 school horses and the premiums cost more than it would cost to replace them. It may be a better business decision to take a loss or two rather than pay premiums to cover these animals.

Tips for Insuring Horses

If you want to insure your horses, there are several ways to keep costs to a minimum:

- Shop around for the best premium. Do not, however, sacrifice quality service, such as prompt claims payment, for a lower premium.
- If your premium is sizable, find out whether you can arrange for a payment plan with a minimal or no service charge.
- If you need to insure a large number of horses, inquire about getting a discount for covering all of them through the same company.
- Ask other horse owners which agents and insurance companies they have found that provide the most competitive rates and best claims services.

Safety Never Takes a Break

- Practice safety in and around the barn and on the horse at all times.
- Require all riders to wear helmets that meet ASTM/SEI safety standards and boots or shoes with heels.
- Hire only safety-conscious, qualified instructors.
- Teach with sound and safe horses.
- Stop and correct any practices that are unsafe.
- Teach students the proper way to tack up, lead, mount, and dismount a horse.
- Teach etiquette and safety on trail rides and when riding in a ring with more than one horse.

Safety equipment can reduce injuries. All riders must wear helmets that meet ASTM/SEI safety standards and sturdy boots with heels.

PROPERTY INSURANCE

Property insurance is vital to your business. Consult with an agent experienced in dealing with farm properties. Make sure your insurance will cover equipment, such as tack, when you are transporting it to shows.

Keep a list of everything your policy covers and its estimated value. Some insurance companies recommend photographing or videotaping insured items to supplement your records; if your policy covers equipment in your tack room, for example, film the tack room when every item is in place.

LIABILITY INSURANCE

If you keep horses primarily for pleasure, some coverage may be included as part of your property insurance. For any type of horse business, however, liability insurance is crucial and, in some states, it is mandatory and may have to be purchased in addition to property insurance. The skyrocketing cost of liability insurance has made operating a horseback-riding stable far more expensive than it used to be. There are ways, however, to help keep down premiums — and minimize the likelihood of getting sued, such as:

- Require riders or parents to sign release forms before you let students mount a horse. Contact a local attorney to obtain the appropriate forms.
- Check with your state horse organizations to see whether they offer any group policies.
- Make sure your agent understands all the various activities that go on at your farm to ensure that you obtain all the types of insurance coverage you need.
- Shop around. Echo Brook Farm, which gives carriage rides, saved hundreds of dollars by going through their local agent for the same amount of coverage the national insurance group had offered.
- Talk to an attorney about how to set up your business so it is separate from your personal account. You may want to set up a limited liability corporation (LLC). This limits your liability. Someone may sue the business but your personal assets are protected and safely out of reach.

INSTRUCTORS' INSURANCE

Make sure that if you are traveling to other barns and giving lessons that you have instructors' insurance. It ranges from $500 to $1,500 per year and covers about $2 million in liability.

Most insurance for equine businesses comes from Agrarisk through Markel. See whether your local insurance agent can go directly and get the same coverage for less.

Integrated Systems

Integrating the various services you provide, such as schooling, boarding, and breeding, will enable you to make the most of your horses from birth to retirement or for as long as you are associated with any horse you handle.

Let's say that you breed your mare to a very handsome Conformation Hunter Stallion. Eleven months later, she foals and you're the proud owner of Royal Ruth, a pretty gray filly. When she's ready for halter-breaking, you set up a short course on how to halter-break a foal. Seven students take the course and not only do you take in their course fees, but Royal Ruth is also now halter-broken.

As Royal Ruth matures, you can offer similar instruction on how to train a horse to longe and break to saddle. The filly impresses one of your advanced students, Laura. You make arrangements to lease her to Laura, who is now paying for leasing as well as lessons. When the mare is ready to show, you can receive the trailering fee and the horse show–schooling fee. Since Laura is paying her own entry fees, Royal Ruth is basically being shown for you free of charge. Of course, you would entrust a young horse only to a capable, experienced rider and handler under your supervision.

Later, Laura moves out of town, and Katie, another student, expresses interest in buying Royal Ruth. Your selling price is more than she can afford so you reduce the price to encourage Katie to buy the horse and keep her on your farm, where you can continue to profit from her. The mare is now a proven show horse; Katie boards her at your barn, continues to take lessons from you, and goes to shows with you.

Don't Be a Victim of Fraud

If anyone even hints that he may have a liability claim against your stable, check out the source of the claim. At a stable where I once worked, a couple came for a trail ride, fell off their horses, and said they were injured. Then, they tried to sue for damages. Mysteriously, their release forms had disappeared. Suspecting foul play, we checked around with other stables and found out this was not the couple's first "accident." In other cases, they also sued and received out-of-court settlements. In the case of the stable where I worked, we insisted on going to trial. We had high attorney's fees, but we won — and had the satisfaction of knowing that this couple did not get away with a fraudulent claim against our stable.

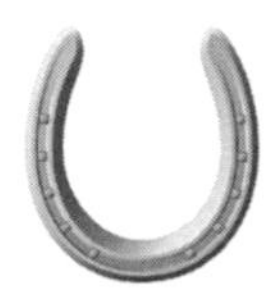

MONEY-SAVING TIP

Consider reducing the sale price of your horse or financing the sale yourself to keep it in your operation. That way you can continue to profit from horses like our example horse Royal Ruth for years to come.

For Christmas, Katie's parents buy her a new saddle and bridle from your tack shop. Her mom decides to take lessons so that she can start riding the horse as well. Now you are receiving board payments, lesson fees, and tack sales from your horse sale.

A few years later, Katie is off to college and wants you to sell the horse for her. Because of Royal Ruth's excellent training and show record, which Katie paid for, the horse's value is quite high. You sell her to Brant, a rider who is new in the area, and you receive a sales commission. He is busy with his job so you offer full board services including grooming, clipping, and exercising. Now you can increase your profits by offering more services in addition to regular board fees. Brant also needs the mare exercised so you offer to use her in the riding school. A cost-free school horse is now available for your riding program.

After some years, Brant decides to breed Royal Ruth. Eleven months later you have a new boarder horse to train and break. The process begins again. After many years of useful service, Royal Ruth retires on your farm, with Brant paying for pasture board for the rest of her days.

This is what I mean by an integrated system. By planning ahead and taking advantage of opportunities, you can get significant mileage out of each and every horse.

From foal in training to competitor to brood mare, a horse can earn her keep in many ways for many years.

PROMOTING YOUR BUSINESS

There are a number of ways to promote your business, and many of them are described in this chapter. Adopt only those that will enhance your business in the immediate future. You can initiate other promotional programs later, as you need them.

Creating an Image

To make your business a success, it must have an image. The image you develop for your enterprise should appeal to current clients and help attract future ones. The following are tools and equipment to help you develop an image and get the word out about your business.

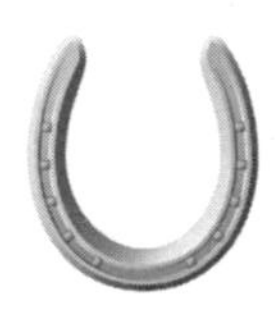

MONEY-SAVING TIP

Consider bartering with an artistic friend or acquaintance who can design a logo. For example, one of my barn workers was a frustrated artist who had dropped out of architecture school. He was happy to spend a day designing a farm logo and I received professional-quality art for farm-labor rates.

NAME YOUR OPERATION

If you haven't already done so, give your farm or ranch a name. Try to select one that people can easily pronounce and remember. Avoid names that could be mistaken for another type of business, such as McDonald's.

Your farm's name should indicate not only that your business is about horses, but also what kind of horse business you operate. Center Line Stables, for example, would indicate a dressage stable, while Rodeo Ridge Ranch would make it clear that the barn is Western. If riding lessons will be the major focus of your business, you may want a name with "school" in the title. For horse businesses that offer all types of riding, a more general name, such as "Springfield Riding Center," would be more appropriate.

CHOOSE FARM COLORS

When selecting farm colors, pick tasteful ones that are widely available. I once made the mistake of choosing terra-cotta and beige for a farm in Texas that I managed. Have you ever tried to find a blanket or halter in terra-cotta and beige? It didn't take long for me to realize that I needed a different color scheme, so I changed to red and white.

When you can, select barn equipment, such as buckets and hay nets, in the colors of your farm, or use colored tape to identify your equipment. This helps you keep track of it at horse shows and other events.

DESIGN A LOGO

A logo is another way to develop an image and promote your business. Unless you happen to be a graphic artist, have a professional designer create your business logo. Explain that you want an eye-catching, memorable logo that defines your business. Ask for one with clarity in design so that the size can be easily reduced for use on business cards or enlarged for roadside signs or banners.

Obtain ownership of the logo so that you can use it freely throughout the life of the farm. If the artist retains ownership, you could be charged a fee each time the logo is used. The initial cost of having a logo designed may seem high, but it's well worth the price once you see how widely it can be used to promote your business.

Put Your Image to Work

Once you have a name for your barn, colors, and a logo, what do you do next? Use them on everything, including brochures, newsletters, letterhead, envelopes, your Web site, invoices, prize lists, posters, and even coolers and blankets. Following are some business tools on which your barn's name, logo, and colors should be prominent.

BUSINESS CARDS

These are essential. Always carry them with you and distribute them freely. Network. Include all pertinent information on the cards but, at the same time, not so much text that they look crowded and unprofessional.

BROCHURES

Your farm should have an attractive brochure that tells readers what it has to offer. Hand out the brochures to prospective clients and keep some in the office, where they will be available to visitors.

Have a professional assist with the wording, layout, and graphics. Before you begin to design it, think about the quality of your product. Do you need a flashy brochure with color photographs, or would it suffice to have a simple but attractive black-and-white brochure with just enough type to sell your goods and services?

POST SIGNS

Once you purchase these business tools and start putting them to use, you'll want to display your barn's name and logo where a larger audience can see it. Signs along the road work well because they put the name of your business before the community and can direct potential clients to your farm.

Here are some pointers to consider when creating and posting signs:

Post signs on your property. If you need to use adjacent land belonging to another party, always obtain written permission. Check with your local zoning board for regulations governing the placement of road signs.

Place signs in plain view near a well-trafficked street, at the intersection of a major roadway, if possible. Smaller signs with arrows will also help steer visitors toward the farm.

What a Brochure Should Say

Your brochure should include the following information:

- Name of your business
- Brief description of your operation
- List of services available
- Names of the owner, manager, and instructors
- Location and map
- Address, phone number, fax number, and e-mail address
- Pictures — the most effective part of any brochure
- Logo and farm colors if it is a color brochure

This eye-catching sign of a horse-shaped figure appears to be jumping out of the pasture.

Make the message on the sign brief, informative, and large enough to be read from a distance. Ideally, it should include the business name, owner, and a phone number. You may want to include some services you provide ("trail rides," for example).

Construct the sign from long-lasting, weatherproof material and embed the supports in concrete to avoid replacing it every few years.

Consider the shape and size of your sign. The most effective sign for a horse operation includes the image of a horse. One of the most eye-catching and impressive signs I have ever seen was in the shape of a full-sized jumping horse and attached atop the property fence. To a driver approaching the farm, the horse appeared to be jumping out of the pasture. As you got closer, you could read the name of the farm, its services, and its phone number on the horse.

Place a sign on the sides of your vehicles. Put your farm name, your telephone number, and your logo on the sides of your cars, trucks, and trailers; either paint it on or use a removable magnetic sign. This way, you are promoting your business wherever you drive, and your vehicles frequent areas you want to target: feed stores, veterinary offices, tack shops, and horse shows.

Although painting the information on vehicles looks more professional and lasts longer, magnetic signs are useful if you don't want your logo permanently affixed to your family car: Teenagers and mothers-in-law aren't always excited about driving around in a car that's advertising horses.

Invest in Good Telephone and Answering Equipment

How many times have you called a horse barn and no one answered the phone? Or the person who answered was unfamiliar with the barn's operation, or didn't take the message correctly? Perhaps when the phone was answered, the horses were neighing, the tractor was running, or the farrier was pounding, and you hung up feeling frustrated. Frustrated callers are left with a poor impression of the barn and may take their business elsewhere.

There are few pieces of office equipment that are as crucial for your organization as an adequate telephone system. If you select wisely, you'll be accessible to current or potential clients, be able to conduct business when necessary, and convey the image of a well-run operation.

Install at least one telephone in your barn as well as in your office. Select quality equipment that will last. Built-in speaker phones allow you to have conference calls with the veterinarian and the client. Portable telephones allow you to have mobility, and cellular telephones and beepers enable someone to reach you in an emergency during foaling season. These can be expensive, so figure out first whether they are necessary and worth the investment.

Don't Let Those Calls Get Away!

When no one is there to answer the phone and messages are left on the machine, schedule a time of day to return calls. Returning calls efficiently promotes the image of a well-run business.

TELEPHONE TIPS

The following suggestions will help you to be more accessible to current or potential clients:

- Have pen and paper secured next to each telephone. Keep your calendar and a list of upcoming events, teaching dates, and horses for sale near the phone to avoid missing any business opportunities.
- Instruct people who answer the telephone to do so professionally. They should state the name of the farm, give their name, and ask how they can help the caller.
- If students, boarders, and visitors to the farm often tie up your business line and run up the telephone bill, consider installing a pay phone for them to use or only make available local service and use a cell phone or calling card for your long-distance calls.
- The answering machine is an important extension of the telephone. Check the recommendations in *Consumer Reports* and buy a machine that will last. It will pay for itself by preventing lost business. An answering machine will allow you to screen calls while conducting other business, and remote-use options allow you to listen to or leave messages from another location. They are invaluable for staff communication ("I'll feed the horses in the morning," or "Expect a feed delivery tomorrow."). Machines that record the date and time of messages are particularly useful when students call in to cancel a lesson.

Proofreading Is Profitable

Always proofread the copy of printed material before it goes to a printer and save your initialed receipt. I once proofed a piece before it went to print and made sure there were no errors. The typesetter then omitted a word. Because I could prove it was the printer's error, I got the material for half price.

- Record a clear, brief, informative message on your answering machine. Change outdated messages promptly. If you receive many calls inquiring about which services you offer, you may want to mention the services you provide on the tape. For example, "We specialize in English and Western riding lessons and weekly trail rides."

Newsletters

Create an annual, quarterly, or monthly newsletter for students, boarders, other farms, feed stores, veterinary offices, and guests to communicate with others and promote your business. Include the successful activities that have taken place at your farm and exciting upcoming events. People enjoy seeing themselves and their horses in print.

Be sure to take lots of photographs of your students with their favorite "horsey friends" and insert them into your newsletter. Have students submit photos and include a "horse photo of the month" in the newsletter. E-mail the newsletter to your listserv of clients and network contacts, and put all issues on your Web page.

If you are printing color photos say, once a year for a holiday newsletter, check the price at your local print shop. It may be able to do it less expensively than you could buy the color cartridges and paper.

You can also include:

- Upcoming riding events — shows, clinics, short courses, and trail rides
- Horses for sale
- Inoculation and worming schedules
- Informative articles, quotes, poems, cartoons, and puzzles
- Special services — clipping, spring blanket washing, trailering services, etc.
- Special awards — rider of the month, employee of the month, emergency dismount of the month, horse or dog of the month
- Tack shop specials
- Barn socials
- Used tack swap day
- Tack cleaning party

Include in your newsletter a contest for "horse photo of the month."

Promotional Material

Remember, the type of promotional material you produce reflects the quality of your business. You want to have the best business cards, brochures, newsletters, and stationery you can afford. Strive for excellence without extravagance; save on costs without sacrificing quality.

- At shows, clinics, or around the holidays, arrange to have a professional photographer take pictures of students and boarders in riding clothes and with their horses. Offer the photographer the opportunity to take individual portraits and sell them to the students and boarders. In return, ask the photographer to provide, at no cost or at a discount, scenes from the farm that you could use in your brochure.
- Comparison-shop for printing. Some printers use colored ink on certain days for the same price as black and white.
- Buy in bulk and get the most for your money. For instance, the cost of printing 1,000 business cards or brochures may be much less per piece than the cost of having 100 items printed at a time. Estimate if you want the supply of brochures, business cards, or other items to last 1 year, 2 years, or more, then order accordingly. Don't include specific prices or schedules of events in promotional materials such as the brochure or they'll soon be outdated.
- Alternatively, you can now buy make-your-own business card kits to create cards on your own computer and printer.
- Get an estimate from an online printing service (see Resources [page 217] for suggestions). They will have tips and uploads. Look for a 1-week (or less) turnaround service and a creative team to design it for you. Many sites will guide you with online suggestions for safe margins, bleed trim marks, resolution, colors, images, layout placement, and more.
- Develop a good relationship with a quality printer and that printer may be willing to donate trophies and/or buy advertisements in horse-show programs.
- You can design calendars, gift certificates for riding lessons, and holiday cards to sell in your tack shop or office as well, all of which will promote your operation.

Get Your Name Out There!

Here are some suggestions for promotional slogans and bumper stickers:

- I jump for Ten Oaks Riding Center.
- Ten Oaks Riding Center is a stable place.
- Let's horse around at Ten Oaks Riding Center.
- My other car is a horse at Ten Oaks Riding Center.
- Have you hugged your horse at Ten Oaks Riding Center today?
- I'd rather be riding at Ten Oaks Riding Center.
- Ten Oaks Riding Center Horse Show Team
- Ten Oaks Riding Center Summer Day Camp
- Ten Oaks Riding Center Riding Instructor
- Ten Oaks Riding Center Staff

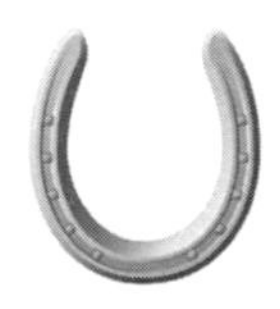

MONEY-SAVING TIPS

Swap goods or services. Perhaps a printer would be willing to trade paper products for riding lessons for herself or her children. (Before bartering, however, see chapter 3, Financial Management, because there are tax implications.)

Get free "advertising" for your farm by sending press releases (with photographs) to your local newspaper. Neatly type up the results of an event or information about an upcoming event, and chances are good that your local newspaper will publish them.

PROMOTIONAL GOODS AND GIFTS

Invest in tastefully designed bumper stickers, T-shirts, sweatshirts, jackets, key chains, baseball caps, sun visors, dog coats, grooming aprons, pens, memo pads, and/or magnets. Sell the more expensive items to cover your costs, and give the smaller ones as promotional gifts to prospective students or boarders. Give them to people from other farms who buy a horse from you so they don't forget your farm name.

Come up with a new slogan every year. Hold an annual contest in which students and boarders provide suggestions, then award a prize for the best one.

Commercial Advertising and Promotion

Passing out business cards, brochures, and newsletters and putting your colors, logo, and Web site address on your signs, equipment, and vehicles will help promote your business, but commercial advertising and promotion also are necessary to ensure success. The primary sources for advertising are newspapers, specialty magazines, telephone books, television and radio, placards and billboards, and the Internet. Following are some pointers for advertising in each medium.

NEWSPAPERS

Newspapers in major cities have the broadest circulation and, as a result, are an expensive place to advertise. Local newspapers or weekly papers are less expensive and, because they often need your advertising dollars, are usually more willing to negotiate good deals. Advertisements in high school and college newspapers, particularly those that have a riding program, are even more inexpensive and may target the specific age group you want to reach; this also promotes goodwill for your business with the students and faculty.

Regardless of the newspaper in which you choose to advertise, take the time to establish a rapport with one person on the staff. Ask this person to inform you about upcoming articles that discuss horses favorably, and advertise in that issue, preferably near the article. To reach newcomers in the area, run a small monthly or weekly ad in the classified advertising section; include a short list of the services you provide, such as lessons and boarding. Always negotiate for the best advertising rates.

THE ALL-IMPORTANT PRESS RELEASE

When writing a press release, you need to consider your goals (building attendance, business, or just name recognition), what facts you want to communicate, and who is your target audience. To promote an upcoming horse show you will need to include what's going on, whom to contact and how, when it is, and where. If the paper allows you the space, explain why someone will want to come to watch and what they will see. Submit the press release at least a week before the show. You may pique the interest of a reporter who will come out and cover the event.

This is the best free advertising you will ever get. It may take a year of sending in press releases and getting to know reporters and inviting then to come out and write an article about your farm programs, but it will be worth the work. Not only will a published account bring in new business, but seeing their names in print can also build confidence, pride, and loyalty among riders at your barn.

After the show be sure to send in the results of the classes, or at least who won the championships and reserve championships, with a brief description of the show as space allows. Remember to include your contact info and Web site.

You can also call the local TV stations to invite someone to cover your show or do a video spot about your operation. Sometimes it takes going outside of our comfort zones and being a bit cheeky to call the press, but taking the initiative will really pay off in the long run.

Invite the press to visit your barn, camp, lessons, clinics, and shows. Perhaps a reporter will want to write a feature article about your farm, complete with photos. This is terrific free advertising. You may get new clients as a result, and press coverage will no doubt be better in the future.

SPECIALTY MAGAZINES

Advertise your horses, products, and events in magazines. Specialty magazines are the most effective since they reach the audience you want to target; you'll get a better return

The Publicity Effect

Here are some examples of how publicity can be good for your business:

- Barbara gets home after schooling her big bay hunter. She sees the write-up on the sports page about the Ten Oaks Riding Center Horse Show. She decides to enter her horse in the next show at the farm.
- Linda has just moved to the area from out of state but hasn't yet moved her horse, Moses. She sees the results from the show in the newspaper and calls the farm to see whether it offers boarding.
- Melissa is in her pajamas, sipping a cup of coffee. She glances through the sports section and notices the results of the horse show. The daughter of her best friend won a ribbon. She decides to sign up her own daughter, Elizabeth, for lessons at the farm.
- Charlie has been looking for a more experienced horse for his wife. After seeing the article, he contacts the farm to see what's available.

Build Goodwill!

If the profit from the sale of a local horse is sufficient, run an ad in your local paper congratulating the new owner. It helps build goodwill toward your farm. It is also one more opportunity to publicize the name of your business with the message that you sell horses.

for your money than you would by advertising in publications that go to a lot of people you do not need to reach. For example, a local children's magazine is a good choice if you are advertising summer day camp or a riding program for children. For advertising horses or horse-related products, run your ad in a horse magazine.

Often, people are impressed when someone selling a horse takes on the expense of advertising in a well-known magazine. I know a horse trader who had been trying to sell a hunter for several months. A few people came out to see the horse, but no one was very interested. The trader then advertised in *The Chronicle of the Horse* magazine and raised the price of the horse to cover the cost. Someone who had rejected the horse before now saw it advertised in this magazine, came back, and paid the higher price.

TELEPHONE BOOK

Day in and day out, you probably will receive more calls from people who have seen your name in the telephone book than any other place. List your name in as many sections and in as many ways as you can in the phone book. The white pages are free. Try to list your name, the name of the farm, the camp, and the tack shop.

The Yellow Pages can be costly. Some people searching for barns will look under "Riding Instruction"; others may turn to "Horses." You'll want to list under both, so negotiate getting several listings for one price, or at least at a discount on the listings.

Check out the ads run by competitors to see what you can do to make yours more eye catching. Print the ad in bold or use a decorative border; both will draw attention to your ad without running up the cost substantially.

Online advertising, however, has outpaced the Yellow Pages and in many areas there is more than one phone book in use, which dilutes your advertising dollar. Do your research on the prices and books in your area and weigh the cost versus the benefits before investing in phone-book advertising.

TELEVISION AND RADIO

The cost of advertising in larger, more well-known television and radio stations is prohibitive for most horse farms. The exception may be public and cable television stations and small, local radio stations. The latter often welcome the opportunity to announce events in their area, and do so free of charge. Routinely send them announcements about activities at your farm. They might even come out and cover your event.

PLACARDS AND BILLBOARDS

Recently I walked into the local shopping mall and was greeted, to my delight, by a sign advertising Harmony Hill Equestrian Center with lovely color photographs of students jumping horses and the Web address of the farm. There was information about lessons and summer camps. The manager of the farm told me the ad cost her $280.00 a month for 6 months and she was monitoring the number of calls she received to see whether it was worth the cost.

The sign had fabulous visibility and was certainly reaching the target audience that most frequents malls and equestrian centers — teenage girls! This might be a potential source of advertising for you, but monitor the return on your investment dollar.

How Much Is It Worth to You?

It is difficult to know exactly how much you should spend on advertising. Don't spend more than you can afford, but be sure to set aside some money for advertising. Build that into your annual budget or, better yet, your business plan. Word of mouth is effective, but advertising reaches thousands of households, many of which may contain horse lovers. This is especially important when you are beginning a business. After years in the business, you may not need to advertise at all.

Computer Marketing

The addition of the computer to your marketing plan is essential. Technology has enhanced our ability to reach people we never thought possible quickly and inexpensively. The following are ideas on how to do your own computer marketing.

WEB SITES

When designing a Web site, many people go to a professional designer. You can find hundreds of them by searching the Internet or looking in your local Yellow Pages, but you can easily create your own as well. With just a little knowledge and the ability to read and follow directions, you shouldn't have a problem. It may not be the fanciest, but you can save hundreds of dollars by doing it yourself.

Pictures Tell the Story

Choose the pictures you want to add and make sure:

- They are good, clear photos that show you and your horse off to the best advantage
- The background is clear and attractive
- Your horse is clean, alert, and standing squarely
- The tack is clean and fitted correctly
- If jumping, the horse's knees are tucked well and even
- If you are in the picture, you look professional, clean, and happy
- If you are riding, check that your equitation won't embarrass you
- Show you are safety conscious by always wearing a helmet when riding

There are many hosts that will give you free Web site access. Whichever you choose, make sure the links work and you can edit and add information and pictures easily. You can buy your domain name for less than $100, and it is a lot easier for people to find your site using your farm name.

To start, type the words "free Web site" into your favorite search engine. Review what each company has to offer and choose the one that is best for you. Next, read the directions of the host you have chosen.

If you plan to create your own, it helps to write an outline of everything you want to add to your site. Include the music that will play while the site is open and your template for all the other pages, with graphics and colors.

Home Page

All of your links should generate from your home page and return to it or to your link directory. Home page elements usually include:

- Several eye-catching photos of your horses doing what they do best (action shots are great)
- A brief history of your farm and your goals
- A mission statement and philosophy
- Contact information! *Don't forget* name, complete address, e-mail contact, and phone numbers
- What are you offering? Lessons and boarding; horses and ponies for sale; equipment and vehicles for sale; clinics, shows and special events; camps?
- Staff biographies
- Location and facilities (maps are great — you may be able to get a free aerial photo)
- A "counter" to learn how many people are dropping by

Links

You can have as many links as you wish. Look at other sites for ideas of what you want on yours. You can add links to breed clubs, friends' sites, and businesses that you recommend.

Check that all the links work correctly. This is very important. People will stop looking at your Web site if the links don't work.

Online Networking

Using computers wisely can be an excellent way to promote, network, and advertise your farm. If you don't have a computer, see chapter 3, page 54 for information. If you have never used one, be brave — the time has come!

Here are some ways you can network through a computer.

E-MAIL

E-mail is a great way to keep in touch with clients and respond to any customers drawn in by your advertising.

Try to check your e-mail at least twice a day, once early in the morning and once at night. Answer all e-mails in a timely manner. Use good time management when you're online. Don't waste precious hours. Give yourself time limits if necessary.

Create a signature that includes your farm name, address, and phone numbers.

GROUPS

There are groups for every topic of interest. If you can't find a group that interests you (on www.yahoo.com and others), you can start your own. You will have to sign up, but once on board, you will probably receive more messages in a day than you want.

Groups are a great way to:

- Network, making new friends and clients who share your interests
- Advertise your animals
- Find out about shows
- Find tack and other items
- Share ideas, concerns, happy and sad events
- Find out about fads in your discipline
- Ask questions of others who are knowledgeable

MAILING LISTS

You can join mailing lists of your favorite trainer, club, or group simply by registering online at each site. Once you have filled out a "membership/join" form and submitted it online, you will receive updates of events and announcements as they become available.

A Professional Web Presence

Nothing looks less professional than a sloppy Web site with typos. Be sure to edit all text for grammar and spelling. Ask a professional or friend to review it. Often when one writes something and reads it over and over, it is easy to skip over the same mistake. It can help to read it backward, starting at the last word and checking until the first.

Through the Internet you can find — or create — a group that shares your interests, from therapeutic riding to "games on horseback."

Web Sites to Visit

The Internet is full of sites that can help you in your business. Here are just a few:

eBay. You can find almost anything you may need on eBay.com: tack, trailers, trucks, show clothes, boots, barn and grooming equipment, and much more. Just watch out for the shipping charges. Some sellers will list an item at a very low price, but their "shipping and handling" fee raises the price so high you could buy it new at your local dealer.

Craigslist. This site sells everything. Go to the farm and tractor link, and you will find everything from tractors to horses and ponies. You never know when someone will have exactly what you want at a great price. Check this one daily if you're looking for a special item.

Tack distributors. Most tack distributors (such as Miller Saddlery, Dover, Valley Vet, Stateline, and Country Supply) have Web sites, and they run "online" specials that you can't get in the store. Join their mailing list and watch for needed items to go on sale.

You can also create an address book and your own mailing list to send items to your friends, family, and clients. This is a great way to send show programs to large groups.

Once a name is added to a mailing list, it will stay until you delete or edit it. Keep your lists updated. With the high cost of postage, they can save you time and money.

BLOGS, FACEBOOK, TWITTER

You can set up a blog to share your interests and invite whomever you want to join in. Alternatively, you can search for other people's blogs about things that interest you.

Consider setting up a Facebook or Twitter account as a way to reach out to a wider audience.

Public Relations

In addition to commercial advertising, there are many other ways to promote and build your business. One of them is to boost public relations by hosting activities.

Here are some ideas:

- **Host camp-outs.**
- **Participate in "career days"** offered by many high schools to acquaint students with stable management or certified riding instruction. Students can come to the barn or a riding instructor can speak at the school.
- **Donate lessons** for a charitable group's raffle or auction. Your donation might be deductible and, ultimately, could bring in more students.
- **Hold a seminar on buying a horse.** Ask a veterinarian to donate his or her time to explain potential problems for which to watch. Ask an instructor to talk about buying a horse to match the rider's experience level. Advertise the seminar at your local community college and high school and charge a nominal fee for attending.
- **Host a party for exhibitors** after they participate in a horse show or clinic.
- **Hold an open house** and have hands-on demonstrations on clipping, tacking up, and riding. For many people, it will be the first time they've ever been near a horse.
- **Hold fundraisers.** Organize a theme horse show such

as a holiday show where all participants bring a horse-related gift of less than $10 to be donated to a local equine rescue league. Or hold a trail ride and donate the profits to charity. I once helped organize a 20-mile ride to Austin, Texas. Each rider got pledges for each mile ridden, and the profits went to World Vision, a relief organization. We raised more than $2,000, which was used to aid earthquake victims in Mexico.

- **Attend international riding exchange programs** to expose riders from other countries to your operation. This will give you an opportunity to host a dinner to bring riders together or, if the riders are qualified, a teaching clinic where they can share teaching methods. (See International Riding Programs on page 71.)
- **Organize parties to paint jumps** or clean school tack. At tack-cleaning parties, hold contests for students to see who can put together a bridle the fastest or have mock inspections for "cleanest tack." Give away inexpensive prizes such as hoof picks or your farm bumper stickers to the winners. These parties will foster camaraderie as students swap horse tales and have fun. Provide popcorn and drinks or have a "build your own ice-cream sundae" bar.
- **Offer a loss-leader program,** such as a session of lessons at below your cost, which may lead to additional profitable business. For example, you can offer a session of lessons to the YMCA at an introductory, reduced rate. After the session is over, some of these students may continue taking lessons at the regular cost.
- **Host mock foxhunts.** (See page 101 for details.)
- **Hold square dances** or scavenger hunts.
- **Host a video night.** Select either educational or entertaining horse-related videos.

What Is a Loss Leader?

A loss leader is a product or service offered by a merchant at below cost to attract customers who in turn will come and buy more products that are sold at a profit. An example is when the grocery store sells milk at a small loss but customers go in and buy other products, so the store ends up making a profit.

Building a User Base

If the horse business is going to survive and be profitable, we need not only to satisfy our current market of clients, but also to expand our clientele to get more people involved with horses. This will require both individual and collective efforts among those in the horse business.

Corral Those Names

Build your mailing list free when you host events. Keep on hand a guest book with your name and logo on it. Put it in an accessible place and ask visitors to sign the book and provide their home and e-mail addresses. This increases the number of contacts on your mailing list.

People enjoy horses for many reasons, including business, sport, and recreation. Recreation accounts for about 80 percent of horse ownership. Around 40 percent of these horses and ponies are owned or ridden by youth. This leads to some obvious conclusions about marketing and the potential for expanding our user base.

You and others in the horse industry can convey to the public, through advertising, promotion, and public relations activities, the message that horses can be enjoyed by people of all ages. Horseback riding is a sport you can begin as an adult and continue to master during your entire life.

Following are a few ways to expand the industry's user base. Once you have reviewed the ideas, get together with others in the industry to talk about them, and discuss how to implement them in your locality and state.

- Do cross promotion with public riding stables where rentals are available with basic instruction.
- Help maintain and support riding areas, trails, and public horse-use facilities, especially in urban and suburban areas. In Virginia we have roadside sponsors who adopt and pick up trash along the roadways. Their names are posted on signs along the route. Horseman could do this as well along the trails. Some state and federal programs give you tax breaks if you help maintain some of their trails. Check with your local officials to find out more on how these programs work.
- Develop and implement urban horsekeeping programs.
- Help recycle good, solid horses from one owner to another or assist prospective new owners in locating sound, affordable, suitable, and safe horses. Stress the importance of prepurchase veterinary examinations. After the sale, try to retain new horse owners as satisfied clients by offering the quality services they need.
- Actively support youth riding programs, such as 4-H, Pony Club, and youth breed association activities. Recruit volunteer leaders to run or assist in the programs, or become a volunteer leader yourself.
- Subscribe to horse magazines, which will keep you up to date on the latest in teaching and training techniques, then donate them to schools or public libraries after

you've read them. Suggest that other riding clubs or farms take the responsibility for doing this routinely in their areas.

- Promote the horse as a source of recreation, fun, and sport that benefits the physical and mental fitness of people of all ages. For example, advertise and promote the horse in media that nonhorse owners read, see, and use.
- Form a club specifically to promote horses. In Virginia, for example, a club called the "Railsitters" promotes horse racing and generates interest in the sport. Membership is open to all age groups and costs about $10 per year. For that price, members receive a newsletter, a membership card, and discounts on special tours to horse farms, training facilities, and racetracks.
- Implement fun horse events that will attract and retain both the riding and nonriding public. Most people enjoy watching a jumper class. A drill team from one barn in Maryland rides in formation to music and puts on shows in conjunction with other events, such as summer crab feasts and holiday horse shows. It is always a hit with both riders and nonriders.
- Educate the public to the fact that people do *not* have to be wealthy to use and enjoy horses. Talk about alternatives to owning a horse outright, such as lease and shared-lease options.

Serve the Community

Participate in programs that permit disadvantaged families and families of average means to become involved with horses. Some stables have initiated an "Adopt a Pony" program; sponsors pay for the cost of the ponies, and inner-city youngsters come to ride them.

Many horse farms have "labor for lessons" programs — students do barn work or groom horses in exchange for riding lessons. I think every child who wants to learn to ride should have the opportunity, and those of us in the horse industry can help make it happen: a true "win-win" situation.

Make sure your signage states what services are available.

FINANCIAL MANAGEMENT

The first step in proper financial management is to set goals. Carefully consider your financial expectations. For the best results, whether you aim to earn your living from a horse business or simply to minimize the costs of a primarily recreational endeavor, set clear goals first and then work toward those goals in a systematic way.

Simple financial techniques can help you implement your goals and monitor your progress. If you cringe over such terms as "budgets" and "financial models," take heart; it is not as difficult as you may think. Careful planning and monitoring help ensure that your horse business at least breaks even or, preferably, turns a profit.

Devising a Budget

To manage your horse activities well, you need a realistic budget to help you monitor your ongoing operations and assist you in making important business decisions.

If you are unfamiliar with budgeting, your horse business is definitely the place to start. A budget will allow you to better plan as well as to track expenses and receipts. Remember, though, that it is more than just a one-time plan for revenues and expenses — it is a *system* for continuous financial record keeping and a method by which to compare actual results with anticipated results. For example, if you want to enter the horse-boarding business, a budget will help you determine your exact expenses so you know what rate to charge boarders to make a profit.

In appendix K (page 211), you will find a sample budget that includes income and cash-flow statements for a hypothetical horse operation. These are the two primary formats used in budgeting (see next sections for details). Appendix K also contains blank forms for your use that you can adjust for your type and scale of operation.

Although forms themselves are helpful, the most effective way to build and monitor a budget forecast is to create a flexible financial model using computer software. Find a model that enables you to expand easily on the type of information you want to track. Consider a software package that also will assist you with budgeting, tax planning, and banking. With that help, you can assess your current financial performance or run an analysis to determine just how your profits are affected by changes in costs, pricing of services, and the addition or removal of certain activities.

Budgeting Lets You Take the Reins

Starting and maintaining a budget takes time and discipline, but the information it yields will give you freedom and power over your finances, instead of the other way around. Fortunately, low-cost personal computers and financial software make it relatively easy for anyone to become a part-time financial whiz. At the very least, they can keep you from dreading budgeting as you would a root canal.

The Income Statement

The income statement is a tool that helps you assess the overall profitability of your operation and, if presented in sufficient detail, determines the viability of individual parts of your business. Your goal should be to develop a system that budgets, tracks, and segregates the separate categories of both revenue and expense. In the example in appendix K, page 211, we look at 18 different possible sources of revenue

Bring In an Expert

As with most financial issues, consult with an accountant or a business consultant to help you set up your system. You will save time and money if your model is set up to make extracting tax information easier.

(perhaps you can develop more) and track 21 categories of expenses (perhaps you can develop fewer!).

FIXED AND VARIABLE COSTS

After you have identified various expenses, group them into at least the two major categories known as "fixed costs" and "variable costs." Fixed costs (overhead costs) are constant over the period of your budget and do not vary or change as activity levels change. The cost of leasing property or your mortgage payment would be a fixed cost. Variable costs are those that change with the level of business. This would include the costs of goods sold by your farm as this will change directly in proportion with the amount of goods sold.

The delineation of fixed and variable costs is a useful concept when analyzing financial results. It helps identify possible earning problems. It can tell you whether you have what is known as a "negative gross profit" (net sales minus variable costs), which means you are losing money even *before* you incur your fixed costs. Once you recognize these problems, you can begin finding ways to solve them. You may need to charge more for the services you provide and reduce variable expenses.

Information provided by the income statement can also help prevent you from inadvertently *increasing* your losses by expanding unprofitable segments of your business. Let's say that, overall, your horse operation is profitable. You decide

Make it a discipline to balance your checkbook and review your budget at the same time every month.

to increase profits by doubling the amount of business you do; however, if you haven't broken down the operation to see which parts of the business are profitable and which aren't, you could end up losing money.

Say that riding lessons, analyzed as one activity, turn a profit. Boarding actually results in a loss of $10 per horse per month. If you double the number of boarders, you'll double your losses. This analysis of your business tells you that you need to charge more for boarding whether or not you choose to expand it.

If expenses are getting out of hand, it is usually easier to find ways to reduce variable costs in the short run than it is to reduce fixed costs. As discussed elsewhere in this book (see chapter 13, "Cutting Costs Without Cutting Corners," page 187), you can reduce these costs through careful use, such as implementing methods of conserving energy or of maintaining equipment to make it last forever.

If fixed costs prove to be your main impediment to earning a profit, either you must significantly increase the total level of your sales and services, such as boarding, to cover your overhead, or you'll need to scale back overhead costs while trying to maintain the same level of business. You could accomplish this by selling fixed assets, moving to a site with facilities that are more appropriate for the size of your business, or even laying off administrative or other staff who do not directly contribute to earnings.

COMMON SIZING

As shown in the summary income statement on page 47, it can be very useful to look at your income statement in a "common-sized" format, which simply shows various activities as a percentage of your total revenue. This approach helps you measure the relative, as well as the actual, contribution of each aspect of your business relative to profits or costs. Just a glance at the percentages shown on a common-sized financial statement can often help you quickly identify activities that contribute to or detract from profits.

For a simple example of how to utilize information from a very basic common-sized income statement, let's look at Ashby's Horse Farm.

Income Statement Insights

Your income statement will reveal just how big a bite taxes are taking from your earnings. Be aware that pretax income for income statement purposes and for tax return purposes may be entirely different, depending on the types and amounts of tax credits and deductions that affect your business.

The first thing the income statement tells Ashby is the good news that she made a $200 gross profit (total revenue minus variable costs) in this year and $100 in net income from sales of $1,000. The common-sized results point out further that Ashby earned a 20 percent gross profit margin (gross profit as a percentage of total revenue) and that she made a 10 percent net profit margin (net income as a percentage of total revenue). She can use this percentage to compare with other horse operations of any size or to compare to her own previous year or future years' results to tell her whether she is improving at making income out of revenue. Ashby might be happy having earned a profit, but she can learn much more from her budget results if she just takes a closer look.

Ashby will discover some surprising things from her income statement, including the fact that her major revenue source actually makes no money at all. Riding lessons break even for Ashby (the revenue and expenses related to lessons are both 43 percent of total and net each other out). Expanding her riding lesson business alone will be a wasted effort unless she can charge more or spend less in the process.

Now, look at tack sales. Although they make up 27 percent of total revenue, the cost of tack is only 6 percent of total revenue; therefore, tack sales are the most profitable line of business for Ashby. Whether she realized it or not, Ashby is really in the retail tack business and giving lessons is not a direct moneymaker. Until she can improve her gross profit for lessons, teaching will simply remain a tool for bringing the customers to her tack store and not the other way around. Although she may love teaching infinitely more than selling tack, she now understands that tack butters her bread much, much more than lessons do!

Finally, Ashby should note that while selling Old Red generated 30 percent of her revenue, she actually lost money on the sale because the cost of the horse was greater than the sale price. Had she not maintained accurate records, Ashby might never have realized that the sale of Red brought about a loss. So, along with expanding her tack business and reducing what it costs her to give lessons, perhaps by using

ASHBY'S HORSE FARM

Summary Annual Income Statement

Revenue		% of Total Revenue
Riding lessons	$433	43%
Tack sales	271	27%
Sale of Old Red	296	30%
Total revenue	$1,000	100%
Expenses — Variable		
Riding lesson expenses	$433	43%
Cost of tack sales	57	6%
Cost of Old Red	310	31%
Total variable expenses	$800	80%
Gross profit	$200	20%
Expenses — Fixed		
Depreciation	$20	2%
Interest on loan	50	5%
Total fixed expenses	$70	7%
Total expenses	$870	87%
Pretax income (Revenue minus expenses)	$130	13%
Income tax	30	3%
Net income	$100	10%

Understanding Cash Flow

Here are some examples of items that do not change income but do affect cash flow:

- Changes in receivables (such as payments owed to you for sales made on credit)
- Changes in inventory (such as purchasing more tack than you are likely to sell in the short run)
- Purchases or sales of fixed assets (such as a truck or land)
- Payment of principal on loans

boarder horses, the numbers also remind Ashby that she should continue to keep good records.

Although Ashby has learned a great deal about her business from her income statement, she has at least one more thing to do before making any final budget decisions. She should take a look at her cash-flow statement, which provides some different and very useful information.

THE CASH-FLOW STATEMENT

Where does all the money go? Will I have sufficient cash this year to carry out my plans? A cash-flow statement can answer some of these basic questions.

The cash-flow statement adjusts the income statement for any noncash income statement items, such as depreciation, which are important for your tax calculation but are not so important for your day-to-day cash management. It also measures those changes in assets and liabilities that do not affect income, but certainly do affect cash and, therefore, your day-to-day ability to keep operating.

It is imperative that you understand the difference between cash flow and income. What most people don't realize is that a successful, growing business can easily run out of cash, even if it's making a profit. How? The earnings are being reinvested in the assets needed to grow the business. A successful business can go bankrupt if, when planning for cash, you do not provide the resources needed to pay creditors on a timely basis.

An example of how a cash-flow crunch can occur during a profitable year can be found in the breeding business. If you agree to offer credit terms on the stud fees to the mare owners (deferring payment until later in the year), you may be short on cash to pay for feed and labor costs associated with the mare's care during the breeding season. Since your employees want to be paid on time, you don't have the option of asking them to defer their paychecks just because the stud fees haven't arrived yet. A solution might be to have the mare's owner pay board and veterinary fees when the service is rendered and reserve the stud fee for the final payment. Just be sure to consider the timing of cash flow in addition to profitability when planning your annual budget.

ASHBY'S HORSE FARM

Summary Cash-Flow Statement

Total Revenue	$1,000
– increase in accounts receivable*	200
Total cash collected from operations	800
– total expenses (including income tax, not depreciation)	$880
– increase in tack shop inventory	100
Net cash after operations	($180)**
– Loan payment on land	50
+ Sale of bushhog mower	200
Net Cash Flow	($30)

*sales allowing deferred payment
** note: ( ) indicates negative number

Let's consider Ashby's Horse Farm again to focus further on this topic of cash-flow management. The cash-flow statement above demonstrates that Ashby's annual results were actually a $30 *drain* on cash even though she made a $100 profit.

Cash Flow and Growth Rate

Although the tack shop may represent Ashby's most profitable business, she will need to be careful how rapidly she grows that business because it will require buying more inventory for her tack shop — and this initially will eat up more cash than it will bring in. Also, unless she is careful not to sell on credit terms, the bills she is owed by customers (receivables) will grow more rapidly than the cash she is receiving.

As her business stabilizes, the growth in the amount of receivables and inventory will cease to be a problem. As long as she grows her business, however, more cash will be locked up in activities like buying new saddles and giving credit terms to customers than in deposits to her bank account. In the cash-flow statement, you can see that the growth of receivables ($200) and inventory ($100) drained $300 in cash from Ashby.

Cash Flow and Fixed Assets

Back in The Income Statement section, we gave Ashby a little grief for selling her horse Old Red at a small loss. Certainly, Ashby cannot base her business over the long term solely on selling horses at a loss. However, from a cash-flow perspective, the sale of Old Red (even below cost) could well have been the right thing to do. The sale of Old Red brought much-needed cash into the business, which, in turn, can now be invested in more tack-shop inventory to help that more profitable business grow. It could also be used to reduce the loan on her farm, thereby further reducing her fixed costs over the long term.

The careful monitoring and planning of cash movements helps a profitable business avoid becoming a cash-poor one.

We learn from the cash-flow statement that, because of the negative $180 "net cash after operations," Ashby had to reduce her fixed assets further by selling an old bushhog mower for $200 to raise more cash. We also learn that Ashby had to make a $50 payment on her land loan. Because it was not an expense — but a reduction of a liability — it was not reflected in the income statement.

Hopefully, Ashby has learned the value of using both the cash-flow and income statements in the future management of her farm!

PUTTING IT ALL TOGETHER

In summary, you need an income statement both to measure the long-term profitability of your overall business and to assess the viability of the various revenue-earning activities. Also, looking at the common-sized income statement on a percentage-of-revenue basis helps make all these issues clear.

Finally, be cognizant of your cash position by utilizing a cash-flow statement so you can avoid a short-term cash crisis while growing those parts of your business that your income statement indicates are worth growing. The careful monitoring and planning of cash movements helps a profitable business avoid becoming a cash-poor one. (Appendix K, page 213, contains an example of a cash-flow statement that demonstrates how cash flow can also be greater than net income. It also contains a blank cash-flow form as a sample.)

What's a Partial Budget?

A partial budget (see next page) is a simple, but very useful, four-step process to help you think through whether a new business idea will contribute to total profit.

Tax Time

If you use some of the ideas in this book, you will be more aware of the money-making areas of your business and be able to turn a profit. The Internal Revenue Service (IRS) requires business owners to show a profit every few years (check with the IRS Web site or an accountant for the latest rules). Otherwise, it may consider the business a hobby, and deductions could be disallowed.

Successful businesses are entitled to many deductions, and you'll want to take advantage of every one you can. Traditionally, donating horses to universities, police departments, and therapeutic riding centers provides tax write-offs for horse businesses. We had a Quarter Horse mare that bowed a tendon. We could not use her in the riding school, so we donated her to Texas A&M's veterinary school. It was beneficial to the students' education, the mare was well taken care of, and it was a nice tax write-off and, therefore, a good business decision for us.

Tax laws change, however, so hire an accountant who is knowledgeable about the laws affecting the horse industry. Ask other horse owners to recommend an accountant. Information on tax laws affecting the horse industry is also available from the American Horse Council. (See appendix L, page 217, for the Web site.)

This is a complex subject, and I am a veterinarian and a horse lover, not a tax expert. One key element in my success in the horse business has been to make sure I have good friends who are tax accountants and computer experts. I highly recommend that course.

What You Have vs. What You Need

Before you start bartering, make a list of your products and services. Then think of people with businesses that offer products or services you need. Get on the phone and locate those interested in bartering for lessons, boarding, and so forth.

Here are some suggestions:

What I Can Offer

- Camp
- Trailering
- Tack
- Board
- Aged manure
- Training
- Consulting
- Lessons

What I Need

- Building materials or fencing
- Feed
- Farrier services
- Printing, paper
- Bedding
- Veterinary, legal, medical services
- Advertising
- Repairs, carpentry

Partial Budget for Testing New Ideas

Many of the ideas in this book will result in profitable additions or useful changes to your current horse operation. But how do you know whether a given idea is suitable for your particular situation? What may be a moneymaker for an operation on the East Coast may not be profitable on the Pacific Coast. How can you know what new lines of business or changes in practice will truly help your unique situation?

A partial budget is the answer. It involves what I call organized brainstorming as you consider:

1. added revenues expected;
2. reduced costs, if any, compared with your current practice;
3. reductions in revenue that could occur; and
4. any added costs to expect.

Finally, you bring these factors together and make an informed decision. A simplified example of how to use this budget appears on the facing page. (See also the sample partial budget form in appendix K on page 216.)

You may wish to draw up several versions of a partial budget for the same proposed activity, using different assumptions to decide whether that new business activity would be viable under multiple scenarios of cost and revenue. If you still net a profit or are willing to sustain a loss for a year or two until that part of the business takes off, then you probably have an idea that is ready to work for you.

Bartering

Many suppliers look favorably on bartering, which can provide business opportunities you might not have had if you were required to pay cash. The barter or trading of goods or services eliminates the need for exchanging money. When services or products of equal value are bartered, you don't need to have the cash up front to pay for them. Bartering may eliminate the need to pay sales tax in your state if products of equal value are exchanged. If you trade a $3,000 horse for a $3,000 trailer, and the sales tax is 5 percent, you might save $150.

When bartering, however, you must still adhere to IRS requirements. According to one accountant, there are two

Partial Budget

The new service or activity being considered:

2-week holiday day camp held weekdays from 9:00 A.M. to 4:00 P.M.

1) Added receipts

(This is added income from the new service, which would include the fee charged for the number of camp students anticipated, after-camp child care, etc.)

Tuition for 20 children at $250 each $5,000

After-camp care 4:00–6:00 P.M. for 10 children at $5 an hour $1,000

Total $6,000

2) Reduced costs

(Any costs that might be reduced by the addition of a new service. If you initiate a holiday camp, for example, you might give regular barn staff a 2-week vacation and have camp counselors take over the feeding of horses.)

3 employees earning $6 an hour @ 40 hours per week $1,440

Total $1,440

(A) Added receipts plus reduced costs $7,440

3) Reduced receipts

(This would be any lost income that occurs as a result of the activity. You might, for example, eliminate weekday riding lessons during a holiday camp because you need the horses for holiday camp students; therefore, you would lose income paid by your usual weekday students.)

10 weekday students at $25 each per week $500

Total $500

4) Added costs

(With the holiday camp, for example, you will have added costs such as salaries for camp instructors and counselors.)

Two additional instructors/counselors to supplement existing instructor staff at $20 an hour for 7 hours a day $2,800

Two instructors for after-camp care 4:00–6:00 P.M. at $10 hour $400

Total $3,200

(B) Reduced receipts plus added costs $3,700

(C) Net difference from the new service or activity
(Subtract Line B from Line A) **$3,740**

questions the IRS agent is likely to ask if your business is ever audited: Did you have income you did not report to the IRS and did you have any bartering transactions? The IRS requires you to report the value of goods and services received; you may be able to deduct what you gave in exchange if it is a business expense, but probably not if it is a personal expense. Carefully track bartering transactions and the value of each transaction and present them to your accountant, who will know the latest IRS rules.

Computer Essentials

Some people prefer Apple, others personal computers (PCs); some desktop, others laptop. It's all personal preference. There are several items that you will want on your computer, however, regardless of the make or model.

- **A word-processing program.** Make sure it is user-friendly and has the toolbars you want.
- **Photo editing.** A real must for promoting your horses, both for sale and in "brags." This program must be user-friendly because, even as a beginner, you'll want to enhance and crop your pictures. You may also need to resize the image for publications and to add to e-mails.
- **An Internet server.** Ask around to see which one in your area your friends use and how happy they are with it. Look for the fastest service you can obtain. You'll also need a user name that promotes you or your business.
- **Farm-management software.** There are many to choose from, each offering something a little different, so find the one that fits your business plan best.

Computers and Software

When you are managing a horse business, your laptop computer is as essential as a pitchfork — it will help you better organize your business and maintain records more easily. There are several inexpensive farm-management software programs available. Check with your local computer store or on the Internet for recommendations.

You don't need the brightest and best all the time. Computers don't last more than a few years and technology changes so fast that I prefer the less-expensive model. Nevertheless, buy one that will meet your needs.

MEMORY

My sister says you can't have enough but, then again, she may be losing hers! Try to figure out how much you are going to need and make sure you can add memory if you need it later. Don't pay for a ton of extra memory or extra features you won't ever use. Remember: As in all farm purchases, cut costs without compromising the function. You don't need to be extravagant when purchasing a computer.

GETTING STARTED

If you're not very comfortable with a computer, take an introductory computer course that will teach you to use your computer for business applications. Computer manuals are often difficult for the novice to understand; however, most computer packages have tutorials to familiarize you with the system.

Here is just some of the important information you can store and maintain on your computer, with proper back-up:

- Employee records including payroll information
- Mailing and e-mail lists that can be alphabetized, updated, and printed as address labels
- Budget plans, cash-flow statements, and general accounting figures
- Horse-show management, including entries, payments, points, prize lists, adds/scratches, refunds, class results, championship and reserve championship calculations, and master sheets
- Horse records such as age, veterinary and farrier schedules, and so forth
- Tax records
- Billings
- Checking accounts
- Graphics for farm brochures, camp certificates, and advertisements

Always remember to back up your records. Develop a back-up system for your data using an external hard drive or an online data-management service. If your laptop gets stepped on by a horse or crashes on its own, you want all of your data to be safe and sound.

With relatively inexpensive PCs and software, sound financial management is at your fingertips. (It's also easier and more interesting than you might think.) Even if you hire an accountant or persuade your spouse to take on responsibility for the day-to-day finances, you'll still need to familiarize yourself with the budgeting process and understand your monthly and annual financial statements.

Photo Processing

Once you have loaded your photo-editing software, experiment with it. There is so much you can do that is not hard and will make your photos look professional. Enhance the color, balance the light, crop the picture, take out the red eye, sharpen the edges, or smudge the background. When you have finished and the picture is exactly the way you want it, use it: print it; upload it to your Web page; put it on your blog; make farm flyers; and place it on your business cards, stationery, or invoices. It's your picture — use it to sell your farm and yourself.

When buying a camera, think BIG: If you want to blow the pictures up to poster size, make sure your camera has 8+ megapixels. Fewer pixels and you lose quality when enlarging.

High-Tech Tools

In addition to a computer, you may want to add a few other technological inventions to your inventory.

CELL PHONES

Cell phones are essential for keeping in touch with clients. Keep them charged and turned on. You won't miss calls or have to wait by the home phone for important ones. Ultimately, you may be able to drop your monthly land line and just use your cell phone to save money.

Always store the number of anyone who calls you on the phone and make a hardcopy to keep at home. A hardcopy comes in very handy if you lose your phone or drop it in a water bucket.

GPS

A global positioning system (GPS) is the most wonderful invention I know of for the horse person. When hauling to a new barn, driving to a show at a new location, or just going anywhere unfamiliar, a GPS can guide you there without you getting lost or having to turn the trailer around on a narrow country road. There are many inexpensive GPS systems on the market that work well.

GPS models are growing more and more sophisticated. They give you directions; find restaurants, gas stations, hospitals, and so on; even estimate the time it will take to reach your destination. You just plug in the address of the place you are going and follow the vocal directions. It's much easier and safer than trying to read a map while driving — and more accurate in a lot of cases.

It is a good idea, however, to repeat the directions back to someone at your destination. Occasionally, especially on back-country roads, the GPS may give directions that actually take longer in that area because of windy roads, hills, and temporary problems such as construction detours.

DIGITAL CAMERAS/VIDEO CAMERAS

Here is the really fun part: taking pictures. The wonderful thing about digital cameras is that you can take hundreds of shots, view them on the display screen, keep the ones you want, and delete the rest. Another advantage is that you can order pictures online and have them delivered right to your door. You can also create a Web album that people can access over the Internet. With a video camera, you can take and edit videos of your horse jumping, running, doing a dressage test, or whatever, and upload it to the Internet or make a link for your Web site.

Shooting Pictures

Out of several hundred photographs, it is not unusual to end up with only a handful of good shots. Horses move without warning, and taking a jumping picture, in particular, takes practice. You catch the horse either taking off or coming down. The perfect shot of the perfect jump takes time, a lot of pictures, and luck.

Even though your camera should have "action" mode and burst for getting action shots, you still have to practice. With digital, you don't have the cost of processing an entire roll of film in the hopes of getting one good shot. Just erase what you don't want and keep shooting. The price of secure digital (SD) cards keeps going down while the storage size keeps going up.

Always keep a couple of extra SD cards on hand. It's horrible to arrive at a show only to find you have left the SD card at home in your computer.

BLACKBERRIES AND OTHER PDAS

A personal digital assistant (PDA), a handheld device, such as a BlackBerry, containing a microprocessor, is wonderful for organization. You can record all of your appointments in this lovely item, and it will remind you the day before, again (depending on how you set it up) several hours before, and then again when you are supposed to be there. It can store information about your clients' birthdays, car models, family member names and numbers, horse information, and more. Whatever you want to remember, you can load it into your Blackberry and then download it onto your computer. It can be your phone, your computer, and your brain.

Before you buy one, however, consider the other costs. My brother-in-law gave one to his wife for Christmas and she said, "Yeah, the gift that keeps on taking." They were paying $68.00 a month for the service. To cut costs, you may be able to eliminate your land line and just have cell coverage. Think all of it through before you sign that contract committing you to monthly payments.

Ten Management Tips

1. Develop a financial forecast using a simple computer model and keep up-to-date financial records. Analyze the resulting income statements to help you to make wise management decisions.

2. Complete and assess your cash-flow statement monthly.

3. Require written boarding, leasing, lesson, and sales contracts. With the help of your attorney, design standard forms to keep on hand, and get all transactions in writing. (Some of the forms you'll need appear in the appendixes.)

4. Establish a tax file and keep all receipts in order for your accountant.

5. Open an interest-bearing, free checking account.

6. Establish a savings and retirement plan for yourself.

7. Send out bills promptly. Give yourself the option of charging interest, such as 1.5 percent monthly, for outstanding balances.

8. Turn seriously delinquent accounts over to a collection agency. Include a clause in your boarding agreement allowing you to sell a horse if board is unpaid for 3 consecutive months.

9. Pay your own bills on time to avoid interest or penalty payments, but don't pay any earlier than you must. Have the money in an account that bears interest, which can really add up. The exception might be companies that give discounts for paying bills early; in such cases, weigh the cost of the discount against the interest you get from your bank account, then decide whether it is more profitable to pay the bill early.

10. Require all payments for services in advance. Ask boarders to pay their board for June by June 1. Ask students to pay for lessons ahead of time, too, which helps ensure they'll show up for each scheduled class. One way to do this is by selling a group of five or 10 lessons at a slight discount so the students commit to and pay for these in advance. Plan lesson blocks quarterly instead of monthly to reduce the number of bills you send out and the money you spend on postage.

PART II

Equine Enterprises

RIDING PROGRAMS, BOARDING, AND LEASING

Horseback riding lessons and boarding horses are the mainstays of many horse businesses. You may choose to do one or the other but, if you do both, the potential for making money may be far greater.

Riding Schools

Offering riding lessons to the public can be enjoyable for you as well as for your students. It's gratifying to teach riders of all ages and levels safety measures and the proper care of horses, and to impart your own philosophy and love for these animals.

There are three important components that will make your riding school profitable as well:

- Qualified instructors
- Reliable school horses
- Organized scheduling

General Safety

Horseback riding can be a dangerous sport; falling off a horse can mean head or back injuries. And one lawsuit for negligence can end an otherwise prosperous business.

Emphasize safety with all instructors. Let students know you won't tolerate any "horseplay." Create a safety code and require strict adherence to its rules.

Here are a few suggestions:

- Always require **ASTM/SEI-labeled riding helmets** for everyone who rides at your farm, whether student or boarder. (This goes for instructors as well.) These helmets may not always be the most attractive, but they have been tested to be the safest. Make sure the hat and harness fit properly.
- Always require that students wear **boots or sturdy shoes** with a heel.
- **Fit the horse and the tack** to the rider. A small child needs a saddle and stirrups that are appropriate in order to prevent potential disasters.
- Keep all school tack **clean, oiled, and in good repair**. Dirty tack, such as stirrup leathers, can rot and is more likely to break with pressure.
- Beginners generally require **one instructor for every two to three riders**. Advanced riders can have one trainer for every six to eight riders.
- Make sure **your beginner horses are unflappable**. Don't risk using a green horse when giving lessons. Constantly strive to improve and upgrade the quality of school horses in your string.
- **Conduct safety drills** with students and instructors. For example, one drill might require each student to ride up to the instructor, recite a safety rule, and ride back to the team.
- It may be necessary to **post signs** in your barn, such as, "Don't feed or pet the horses; they might bite," or "No smoking." Speed limit and "Horse Crossing" signs are also helpful.
- Require riders going on trail rides to **travel in groups of at least two** and, when possible, advise them to carry a cellular phone in a fanny pack.
- Enforce a policy of **no alcoholic beverages** allowed on the premises. Drinking alcohol and horse handling are a dangerous combination.
- If you have much activity in and out of your barn, you may want to **make the traffic "one way"** — have one entrance just for incoming traffic and the other for outgoing traffic.

See chapter 5, Riding Camps, pages 79–81, for more on safety practices and procedures.

INSTRUCTORS

Find instructors interested in teaching all levels of riding. Some scoff at teaching beginners, and some barns don't even offer beginner lessons. They may not realize that they're losing tremendous profit potential because many of those beginners will be the dedicated students and boarders of the future.

Strive to find instructors sensitive to the needs of anyone interested in horses. Lessons should be educational and fun, particularly for beginners and children. Adults, of course, will need lessons planned for their level of maturity.

It is important that instructors have a plan for each lesson and short-term and long-range goals for their students. Telling students day after day to keep their heels down and their eyes up can get boring for instructors and students. Have a variety of teaching tools in your mental toolbox, and a somewhat uniform curriculum. Remember to provide guidance for substitute instructors. There are many books available that give ideas for classes. An example is *101 Arena Exercises* by Cherry Hill. Send instructors to an instructor clinic. Watch videos together to find fresh teaching ideas and keep your staff interested.

When beginning students are around, there should be ample staff to help them handle the horses. New riders obviously want to be around horses, but can be intimidated until they learn just how to work with the animals, which may take weeks or even months of lessons.

Horse *and* People Skills Needed

A local riding instructor gave me this advice on riding schools: Be honest with yourself. If you love horses and don't really like people, a lesson program is not for you, so hire good instructors who love both horses and people.

Teaching is not just about the horses: it is mostly about the people who are paying to learn to ride. Without good people skills, you are sunk before you start. Here are some tips.

- When you hire instructors, be sure they are good with all ages and focused on safety.
- If you pay them well, you can pick the best.

- Instructors teaching beginners do not have to be "experts" and top-level riders themselves, but they must be good, sensible riders with a love of horses and people.
- Pony Club, 4-H, and/or British Horse Society Instructor background helps.
- Instructors for the more advanced riders need more experience and expertise and will, therefore, cost more to give lessons.

At our facility, we hire many of our instructors from Virginia Tech — students who meet the needs of the beginner-to-intermediate riders. For the upper level, we have a clinician come in monthly to teach more advanced lessons.

For many of these early lessons, have students pair up. Here is a suggested curriculum for beginners during the first several classes:

1. Show the facility from the tack room to the bathroom.

2. Demonstrate how to groom, pick feet, bridle, saddle up, and lead the horse.

3. Practice proper mounting and dismounting.

4. Have students work in pairs to lead each other on the horse while the instructor teaches the proper position and basic aids, such as halting.

5. Teach students how to untack horses and put away tack properly.

"People-oriented" instructors are essential for a riding stable.

Top-Notch Teachers

Qualified instructors must have not only knowledge and experience with horses and riding, but also the patience and communication skills necessary to pass proper skills on to students with varying levels of ability.

Make Safety Second Nature

Is there an emphasis on safety or a wild "cowboy it" daredevil attitude prevailing on your farm? It's essential to have safety awareness become second nature for everyone you work with. If your instructors are getting lax, they will benefit from a safety tune-up, such as a talk by a local orthopedic surgeon with current statistics regarding injuries to riders.

See chapter 5, Riding Camps, page 76, for more on preparing your staff for an emergency.

SCHOOL HORSES

School horses are the bread and butter of a riding school; therefore, their selection, care, and training are of tremendous importance. The least expensive horses to use are the ones you don't own or pay to maintain. To reduce expenses, ask if any boarders in the barn would let you use their horses for lessons in exchange for a reduced board bill or a few free lessons. Often, it can be a welcome arrangement for boarders who want their horses to get regular exercise but don't have the time to provide it themselves. It's especially helpful to "borrow" horses instead of buying them when you need them for a short period of time, such as during camps.

When you do buy horses, keep in mind that certain types are less expensive to maintain, particularly over the long haul. For instance, a short, stocky grade horse tends to be an easy keeper and is more likely to stay sound lesson after lesson. This saves money compared with a Thoroughbred, which can be more expensive to feed. Ponies are less expensive to purchase and maintain than are horses and may not need shoes. Obviously, you need a few big horses around to teach the older and taller students and a few "fancy" school horses to take to shows. But, overall, particularly for beginner and intermediate riders, the horses don't have to be large, attractive, or expensive.

Be sure to carefully demonstrate the basics like grooming, bridling, saddling, and bathing.

Every year, reevaluate your string of horses and identify those that are proving to be a problem. Some just need time off; others should be sold. I have a rule with school horses: Three strikes and they're out, no matter how good they are on a day-to-day basis. If a certain horse kicks another horse during a lesson, a month later throws a rider, and then a few weeks later, bites someone, he gets sold. Even if the horse is an excellent one for beginners most of the time, the harm he could cause when he's occasionally bad is not worth the risk.

Beginner horses must be unflappable. Beginning riders are your best long-range source of income, assuming they enjoy themselves and continue to move up to the next level and start showing. They need a dependable horse they can trust to build their confidence.

Take good care of school horses. This is essential if you want them to serve you well and maintain a good reputation for your barn. This includes making sure they are routinely inoculated, shod, and fed properly. Sick, lame, or thin horses always cost more to nurse than horses properly maintained along the way. You also are likely to bring in more business if your horses are healthy looking and clean instead of thin and dirty.

Train school horses for the appropriate level and type of riding. Instead of training a horse to be used in the jumping classes yourself, get one of your advanced students to do it. Either have her lease the horse until he is ready to go into the school or, under your supervision, let the student take lessons and train him during lessons. Not only does this get the horse trained, it also gives the student the valuable opportunity to learn how to train a horse and observe his progress.

Periodically "tune up" school horses. Even the best of them can get a little disobedient or confused because of incorrect signals naturally given by beginners. Have your advanced students ride the beginner horses for a lesson and have them perform various obedience drills. This will teach the students how to reschool horses, and it will get the horse back on track.

Beginning Horses

The best beginner horses we have are grade horses of Quarter Horse, Appaloosa, Arab, or Paint crosses. Few Thoroughbreds make the basic beginner-lesson-horse cut here. Warmbloods and "papered" horses are often way too expensive to be a lesson horse.

Remember that, although you need appropriate mounts, you have to be able to get your cost back out of them. It takes a long time to teach enough lessons to pay back an expensive horse. Donations can help, but watch what you are getting: You don't need someone else's problem horse.

Horses Need Vacations, Too

Give school horses a vacation from time to time. Just like people, horses can get sour from doing the same routine day after day. Turn each one out for several weeks during your slower seasons.

Choosing Horses for a School Program

The Harmony Hills manager adds these tips from her own experience about school horses:

Have a strong base group of horses of your own that you are in control of, and pick them for their temperament and patience. They are not always the "pretty" horses. Pretty is as pretty does and is not always the best on which to teach. Have a range of mounts but, most importantly, have a number of great safe, beginner horses. These are worth their weight in gold! Then, you need a few "moving up" mounts at different levels on which more advanced riders can grow.

Find easy keepers. Pass on the hard keepers or sell them before they eat you out of stable and home. Constantly reevaluate your herd. When it comes close to retirement time, when they start to get "a hitch in their giddy-up," find them a good home before they are no longer rideable. I sell some of my older mounts quite cheaply to homes that need a good, safe horse. Recently, we sold a 20-something-year-old serviceably sound gelding for $800 to a family with younger kids who needed a horse to learn and play on. He got a great home and job for his semi-retirement, and we do not have to put him in a retirement field and pay expenses on him.

You can supplement your program with some well-qualified mounts owned by your students, but be sure your insurance covers it, and be sure it is clear in a contract what the "payback" for the owner is and how much that horse can be used.

Don't be afraid to look at the older mount as something you can spend a year training if it has the right temperament. Some of our best mounts have come from someone's backyard and are just "nice" guys. We trained them and then reevaluated them for teaching. If they make good teachers and meet a need in our program, they have a job; if not, we sell them. They need to have the temperament to be teachers — respect the calling God gave them.

If they need training, remember: You have to put the training on them *before* you teach on them! Beginners don't belong on these green horses and will only increase your risk of liability, not to mention the effect on the poor horse trying to learn his job. (I fully agree with this statement and like the phase, "Green and green make black and blue!")

Take care of your school horses. Keep your horses mentally healthy. Give them a variety of things to do. Set your program up, if possible, to do a variety of activities. Even if you teach only dressage, hunter, eventing, and/or gymkhana, have fun days where you play at other things — games, trail rides, polocrosse, trail class activities, and so on.

Keep horses turned out 24/7 if possible. It is better for them mentally and physically. They do fine in the cold and heat with basic shelter and a blanket. (We are the ones who have trouble!) Those not accustomed to full-time turnout quickly learn to love it if given a chance to adjust to it. They may get bleached out, fly-bitten, and dirty, but they are much healthier, less spooky, and more focused when they come in to work. Also, this significantly reduces the cost of stall maintenance: bedding, damage, labor to clean and repair, and so on.

ORGANIZING LESSONS

Organization is the key to a successful and efficient riding program. To simplify scheduling and reduce paperwork, consider offering lessons in quarterly sessions instead of weekly or monthly, such as:

Fall Session: September through December

Holiday-Break Camp

Spring Session: January through May

Summer Session: June through August

Summer Day Camp: Two-week sessions require less paperwork than 1-week sessions

Be sure to keep all medical records and release forms on file so you don't waste paper and time refiling new forms for the same students every session. (See the Camp Form — Sample Camp Application in appendix E, page 200, and Student Record in appendix D, page 199.)

After-School Lessons

Obviously, weekends and after school are prime times for your younger students to take lessons. Organize your schedule to fit in as many lessons as possible after 3:00 P.M. and

Sample Schedule

3:30–4:00 P.M.
Students arrive, groom, and tack up.

4–4:50 P.M.
Lesson

5–5:50 P.M.
Second group of lessons

After the students are finished, they return the horses to their stalls, loosen the girths, and remove the bridles and hang them outside the stalls.

6:15 P.M.
Adult students coming from work arrive, put bridles on their horses, tighten up the girths.

6:30–7:20 P.M.
Lesson

7:20–7:30 P.M.
Students return the horses to their stalls and untack them.

Extracurricular Activities

There are tons of possibilities for fun variety in lessons:

- Want to teach a rider to do flying lead changes? Try pole bending!
- Need to increase students' confidence while trotting? Have them barrel race!
- Need to work on balance and relaxation? Try Pony Club games!
- School horses getting bored? Trail ride in the fields!

on weekends. Students should learn how to groom and tack up their own horses and to untack them and put them away. If time is short, however, have your staff groom and tack up the horses in advance.

During fall and winter sessions, you may only have 2 hours of daylight after school to teach, say, from 3:30 to 5:30 P.M. The horses can already be tacked up for the first set of students, who ride from 3:30 to 4:20 P.M. The next set of students can ride the same horses from 4:30 to 5:20 P.M. These students can untack the horses. Note: You may find it a worthwhile investment to install lights to allow for later lessons during winter months.

THE FINANCIAL SIDE

Have students pay for the entire session, or at least half the session, in advance. Give a discount if they pay up front for the entire session. You'll have fewer bills to send out, and you collect interest on the money received in advance.

Obviously, the group lesson pays the highest dividend per 1 hour of your time; therefore, you should not offer private instruction when you could be holding a group lesson. Private lessons are, however, good moneymakers to fill in gaps between group lessons.

The manager at Harmony Hills says, "Keep good financial records. Without knowing the costs, you cannot set prices that will cover them!" In charging for lessons, I have found that having students pay by the lesson is a tough way to go. Clients need to support the farm if it is to continue, even if they don't feel like riding in the cold. That's why it's essential to establish a cancellation policy.

CANCELLATION/MAKEUP POLICY

Prepare a daily chart of riders and their horse assignments. Students check off their names; the instructors double-check the list for accuracy. Record this on your master chart or computer so that you can accurately track makeups and cancellations.

Make it your general policy to teach rain or shine. You might establish a principle that the stable shuts down only when schools are closed because of hazardous weather.

Lesson Options

One-hour group lesson with seven students in a class	@ $35/student = $245
Semiprivate lesson with two students	@ $50 = $100
Private 1-hour lesson with one student	@ $75
One half-hour private lesson	@ $50

When the stable is open but the weather is too severe to teach outside and you don't have an indoor ring, prepare an interesting ground lesson. This is less time consuming than calling all students to cancel a lesson because of the weather or having 50 mothers call in to see whether you are teaching.

Limit the number of lessons that students can miss and then make up. Require that they cancel at least 24 hours before their lesson so that, if possible, you can find someone to take their place. If they cancel their makeup lesson, offer no further makeups.

VIDEO CAMERAS

A video camera is an excellent training tool. Record a class session and let your students actually see when their heels aren't down or when they duck to the side over a fence.

Videotaping courses and flat classes at horse shows can be a financial opportunity. Set up a booth at the shows where competitors can sign up and pay to have their classes recorded. After the class, let them view or buy the DVD or tape. (See the DVD Order Form in appendix G, page 202.) The same can be done with still photography. Most people send videos online these days but some may still prefer a hard copy.

Use Video Clips as a Sales Tool

DVDs can also be used to sell horses. Send them to potential out-of-state clients who might not drive all the way to your farm. E-mailing pictures and videos or having links from your Web page are great ways to expose your sale horses to a larger number of potential buyers.

Therapeutic Riding Programs

Horseback riding lessons for those with special needs can be a wonderfully therapeutic experience for all. The lessons build motor skills and confidence for the students, give great joy to instructors and volunteers, and provide good public relations for the barn.

The main ingredients for a successful experience are unflappable horses and plenty of volunteers (usually three per rider). Depending on the degree of the disability, you may need special equipment, such as a wheelchair ramp, stirrup covers, and handhold and safety straps.

In some areas, you can set up a program with city parks and recreation agencies. They provide professionals with expertise in working with people with disabilities, and you provide the equestrian teaching knowledge. At one ranch where I worked, we won a mayor's award for meritorious service for our therapeutic riding program. We received publicity and a plaque that impressed visitors. Many of the volunteers and parents of students in the program later took lessons.

For more information, contact the Cheff Center (see appendix L, page 217).

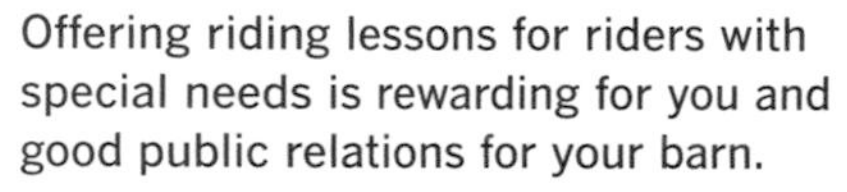

Offering riding lessons for riders with special needs is rewarding for you and good public relations for your barn.

Boarding

My father owns a small apartment complex. He gets calls in the middle of the night from people complaining that neighbors are having a party, the faucet is dripping, or someone is illegally parked in their parking space. Having the title "landlord" in an apartment complex can be a thankless job. In contrast, walking into a barn in the morning and hearing whinnies and neighs from your stable of horses before the breakfast feeding is quite nice. These tenants will never call you "landlord."

Boarding other people's horses can be fun and advantageous or frustrating and unprofitable. First, figure out what level of boarding you want to provide. Some farms rent out the facility but leave almost all other care, including feeding, up to a cooperative of boarders. That type of farm will charge less than a farm that provides all labor and management.

PRICING

To ensure that boarding will be a profitable endeavor, conduct a price sensitivity analysis: Figure out what it will cost you, then what you need to charge to earn a profit. You'll want to be competitive with other farms in the area, so check to see what they charge. Keep in mind, however, that knowing what competitors charge does not tell you their costs. Their farms might not have a mortgage, or maybe they are not making a profit.

When determining a monthly charge, consider the type of clientele you want to attract. A barn specializing in training highly competitive hunters and jumpers or dressage horses will be able to charge considerably more than a barn that appeals primarily to trail riders. Be prepared, however, to offer a higher quality service for the higher price. For example, for the hunters and jumpers, you may have to put on bell boots when turning horses out, add feed supplements during periods of heavy training, and put blankets on and take them off during winter months.

Once you've determined what set of prices can lead to a profit, the next step is to attract the clients. See chapter 2 for principles and techniques of advertising and promoting your business.

International Riding Programs

You may have seen advertisements for "Fox Hunting in Ireland," "Trail Rides in Wales," or "Pony Trekking in Lesotho, Africa." This kind of enterprise also works in reverse. Offering people from other countries the opportunity to see North America from horseback can be big business. If you have the accommodations, an inviting setting, and a heart for internationals, this could be a profitable venture.

International horse publications would be the best place to promote your program. For more information, contact J. A. Allen and Co., a noted British equestrian publisher, which operates the Horseman's Bookshop in London. (See appendix L, page 217.)

Offer What Your Clients Want

Strive to accommodate the riding styles of your boarders. If you have both pleasure and horse-show riders at your barn, don't conduct just horse shows. Organize some fun trail rides or other low-key events as well.

BOARDING BASICS

To hold on to the clients you have once your boarding business is under way, keep the following guidelines in mind.

Make sure your barn is always clean and orderly. Boarders get upset when they pay you to clean stalls, only to find their beloved horses standing in dirty stalls with inadequate bedding. Muck out stalls *daily* and keep bedding clean and comfortable. Strip stalls as often as needed to keep them clean, but as seldom as needed to save on bedding and labor costs. The frequency of stripping will vary according to the individual horse and the type of flooring.

Make sure horses have fresh, clean water available at all times. I once lost a boarder because her horse never had water in his bucket when she came to visit him. Samson, the horse, was watered daily at the same times as all the rest of the horses, and then an additional two times. As Samson drank, he would take a few sips then flip his bucket, spilling the water. I told my staff to be on special alert regarding his water supply, but the owner was concerned that her horse was being neglected and left the stable.

In retrospect, I realized there was a solution. Samson could have been watered from a bucket that could be removed for cleaning, but otherwise was wedged into a corner-mounted feed pan that the horse couldn't budge.

If you also give riding lessons, balance the needs of boarders with students using school horses. Students may resent it if they are distracted from lessons by boarders exercising their horses, and boarders become frustrated if they have nowhere else to ride except an indoor arena where lessons are taking place. Prevent the two groups from getting in each other's way: When the weather is bad, post the student lesson schedule so boarders can plan to ride when the ring is relatively uncrowded.

You might set aside a few hours a week in winter when the indoor arena is "for boarders only," to make them feel as though you are looking out for their riding needs as well.

Demonstrate that you are a professional. Display in your office any diplomas, certificates, or trophies you've earned, which will give students confidence in your abilities.

Clients are more likely to view your business as well run if the barn is orderly and well kept.

Show genuine concern for every horse in your care. Never disparage boarders or their horses. Even if they are criticizing their own horse, don't join in; it can come back to haunt you.

Require payment for boarding in advance (see chapter 3, Financial Management). If this is not possible, don't let anyone get too far behind. Put a clause in the boarder's contract stipulating that you have the right to sell her horse to pay back board, but try to work it out. You could use the horse in lessons or lease the horse, or have the owner work for you to pay off back board. Be compassionate, but also practical.

Leasing

When a horse is conveyed to someone for a specified term and rent, it is a "lease" arrangement. An exclusive lease provides that the lessee is the only person permitted to ride the horse. (See the Equine Lease Agreement in appendix C, page 198.) These leases work well for any of the following:

- Advanced students who are allowed to lease green horses or horses for sale, allowing you to earn money while getting your horse schooled and shown
- Beginning riders who are not yet ready to own and need a less-advanced horse
- Students who are "between" horses.

Leasing often provides riders an opportunity to ride a higher quality or more experienced horse than they could afford to buy.

Instead of being exclusively leased, a good school horse can be more profitable if it is "partially" leased. A partial lease means that the lessee has use of the horse for a certain period of time, such as Wednesdays from 9:00 to 11:00 A.M., or on Mondays, Wednesdays, and Saturdays, for example. This enables you to continue using the horse in your lesson program while also receiving lease payments.

"Lease to Own" is an agreement that enables a rider to purchase a horse over time. First, a selling price is established and then the horse is leased for a certain period of time. When the time period has expired, the lessee may apply the lease amount paid to the purchase price of the horse. The lessee, however, is under no obligation to purchase the horse.

Another variation on leasing is a horse-sharing program. Riders pay a flat fee per month for access to all horses in the program. They can ride any horse in the program they choose, as long as no one else has signed up first to use the horse at the same time.

Extra Services Rendered

Many horse operations are struggling to make a profit without realizing the business opportunities available from offering additional services to their students and boarders. Consider the following financial opportunities for your operation.

- **Grooming** — brushing, bathing, mane pulling, braiding, trimming (muzzle and ears), body clipping
- **Cleaning** — tack, blankets, bandages, trailers
- **Training** — exercising, longeing, halterbreaking, saddlebreaking, showing, driving, hunting, jumping, trailer loading
- **Sales** — leasing, multiple partial leasing, buying, selling, trading
- **Boarding** — full board (include grooming and exercising), regular board (stabling, feeding, and watering), pasture board (boarded in pasture and fed grass and hay only), additional turnouts, lay-ups (boarding and treating injured horses), geriatric board (taking care of retirees), brood mare board (special mare care and foaling check), stallion board (breeding)

Partial Leasing = Profits

Multiple partial leases can be quite lucrative. For example, if you have eight riders who want to lease certain horses for 1-hour sessions on certain days:

Rider A rides seven days a week @ $12/ride =	$336/month
Rider B rides three days a week @ $17/ride =	$204/month
Rider C rides three days a week @ $17/ride =	$204/month
Rider D rides three days a week @ $17/ride =	$204/month
Rider E rides twice a week @ $22/ride =	$176/month
Rider F rides once a week @ $27/ride =	$108/month
Rider G rides once a week @ $27/ride =	$108/month
Rider H rides once a week @ $27/ride =	$108/month
Monthly income from multiple partial leases =	$1,448.00

- **Judging** (get your United States Equestrian Federation judge's license)
- **Teaching** — clinics, seminars, short courses, demonstrations, talks
- **Transportation** — hauling horses and students to and from horse shows, and/or pickup and drop-off service for students taking lessons
- **Catching and holding fee** — when the veterinarian or farrier arrives
- **Consulting** — barn management, horse-show management, farm and horse purchasing, agriculture, course designing
- **Medications** — first-aid treatment (ointments and sprays) and wrapping legs, "Bute," colic treatments, dewormings. Lock the supply cabinet and make sure to charge for the use of these products. Some stables charge an annual fee of about $75 to each boarder, which automatically covers any nonprescription medications provided and administered to horses. Others charge each time they administer medications to a horse.

RIDING CAMPS

Although it takes a lot of work to conduct a horsemanship day camp in the summer or a short camp during the holidays or spring break, these can be great fun and big money earners. You can also organize special-interest camps or clinics, such as a dressage clinic or roping camp, or you can combine horsemanship with other themes, such as an equitation/etiquette camp, or an equestrian/computer camp.

This chapter focuses on summer riding camps for children. The fees you charge will depend on the going rates in your area, which generally vary from $250 to $500 per week for each student. If you teach 20 students a week for 12 weeks per summer at $350 per student, the gross earnings will be $84,000.

KEEPING COSTS DOWN

The two major costs associated with camps are the horses and the staff salaries. To reduce the cost of the horses, use as many boarder horses or borrowed horses as possible. Cut staff costs by allowing the counselors/instructors to ride school horses free of charge each week or take riding lessons in exchange for some of their work hours. If you are able to reduce these costs, you can expect to net a healthy profit margin.

Organizing Camp Sessions

Determine the length of camp sessions and daily hours. You could run 1-week or 2-week sessions during the months that schools are closed; 2-week sessions require half the paperwork of 1-week sessions.

A good length for a camp day is from 9:00 A.M. to 4:00 P.M. This allows enough time for campers to ride both in the morning and in the afternoon — because this is a horsemanship camp, parents will expect their children to ride as much as possible.

Although day-camp activities might officially cease at 4:00 P.M., some parents may not be able to pick up their children until later, after they get out of work. For these children, plan a relaxed, nonequestrian program and charge

The first lesson should be all about bonding with the horse.

Plan for Different Age Groups

If you have both very young campers and teenagers, organize activities for each age group separately because their interests and abilities differ.

an additional fee, or have them work on the farm mucking out stalls, sweeping, or cleaning tack to keep them busy and learning.

If you have a substantial number of campers, carefully consider how you organize their riding time. You can have all the students riding at the same time, which is horse- and ring-intensive, or you can break the campers into groups and have lectures and demonstrations for one group while the other group rides. The latter method reduces the number of horses you'll need and, consequently, the cost of operating the camp, but it requires planning for the lectures.

LUNCH SERVICE

Decide whether you want to require all campers to bring their own lunches and beverages daily, or if you want to give parents the option of paying you for providing meals. Parents with hectic work schedules might be willing, and indeed eager, to have you provide a boxed lunch for their children: a simple but nutritious sandwich, fruit, and a fruit drink. It may be too much work for your staff to take on this responsibility, however. You might be able to have a catering service or local deli provide lunches. Add a nominal fee for your time spent setting up the lunches.

Planning Tips: Countdown to Camp Time

Five months before your first session:

- Send brochures about summer camp to all regular students and horse-show and clinic participants. Begin running monthly ads in the local newspaper. (See chapter 2 on advertising and promotion.)
- Put up posters at nearby elementary and junior and senior high schools. Send an application for the camp to those who respond to your advertisements. (See Camp Form — Sample Camp Application in appendix E, page 200.)

Two months before camp begins:

- Plan the camp schedule, devise a curriculum (page 81), and arrange for the counselors and a director. The ratio of counselors to campers depends on the riding levels of the students. Beginners generally require one counselor for every two to three campers; advanced riders can have one counselor for every six to eight campers. Fewer counselors means reduced labor costs; however, don't sacrifice safety and your reputation by hiring fewer counselors than needed.

- Appoint a director to be in charge of delegating responsibilities to the various counselors. These duties include scheduling activities, assigning horses, receiving payments, making sure liability release forms are signed before each rider begins camp, and anticipating and solving small problems that arise.

The week before camp starts:

- Conduct a training session for counselors and your director. Thoroughly discuss the schedule, objectives, safety rules, and individual responsibilities. It is best to have a separate staff perform the barn work — feeding, watering, and mucking — and have the counselors handle the camp. If labor is in short supply, however, you can have the counselors do the barn work before and after camp, or you could develop a "working barn management camp" for advanced students, putting them in charge of much of the work.
- Compile a task chart to make sure all jobs are assigned, such as filling the drink machine, making sure the water jug is filled, and watching every single camper until he or she is picked up by parents. Have counselors rotate tasks each week. This way, the work is shared equally and no one gets bored with the same chore all summer. It also provides a way for staff members to gain experience handling a variety of duties.

Liability

To protect your horse business, it is imperative that all riders who patronize your barn sign a liability release form. Liability laws do vary, however, from state to state. Consult with an attorney in your area who is familiar with equine business issues and can provide the liability forms you'll need.

Camp Safety

For the sake of your campers' well being, their parents' peace of mind, and the horses, you must stress from the beginning that safety is a priority at your camp. (My husband quotes the sayings, "Horses are dangerous at both ends and uncomfortable in the middle" and, "The only thing hard about riding is the ground!") Horseback riding can be a very dangerous sport, resulting in permanent injury and death, so you need to have a proactive plan concerning safety at

Stay in Close Touch with Your Staff

Staff meetings should be held weekly so that problems can be addressed, which keeps up morale and improves the quality of your camp.

the camp from the first hour. Here are some elements you should have ready.

- A written, posted plan for what to do in case of an accident. Rehearse this with staff and campers.
- A disaster preparedness plan for your farm that instructors know and can carry out. Rehearse with staff.
- Cell phone and work numbers for both parents, regularly updated (not the ones from the release form they filled out two years ago!).
- Release forms and permission slips from parents (authorizing medical treatment), along with campers' insurance information. Keep this organized and readily available in case there's an accident and parents can't be contacted.

BASIC CAMP RULES

Campers need to know that there are boundaries. Print out, distribute, and post in several places camp safety rules that are strictly enforced. Have instructors review them frequently.

These rules might include:

- No running or yelling around the horses.
- No eating, drinking, or chewing gum while riding.
- No jewelry is to be worn.
- Boots and helmet must be worn whenever mounted.
- Horses are *never* to be left in stalls with bridles on and, unless an instructor needs them for the next lesson, should not be left in stalls with their saddles on.
- Campers must lock stall doors after putting away their horses.
- A counselor must be notified immediately of any injury to horse or rider, or of damage to equipment.
- Always notify counselors of an early arrival or a late departure.
- No camper is to leave the immediate premises, ever, unless on a supervised outing.

Riding rules might include:

- Enter and leave the arena in single file.
- Keep at least one horse length between riders.
- Be aware of other riders and their horses, so you have time to respond.

- Do not cut anyone off.
- When approaching one another in the ring, riders should pass left hand to left hand.
- Horses working at a faster pace are given priority to use the outside track of the ring.
- If there is a "runaway horse" all riders must move to the center of the ring and halt.
- If you must adjust your equipment, move to the center of the ring.

STUDY UP FOR AN EMERGENCY

On the Internet you can find comprehensive first-aid courses designed for horse owners and equestrian facility personnel. Use your favorite search engine to select the courses you and your instructors can take to earn the certificate. Online topics include how to prepare an emergency plan for your horse, family, home, and barn; equine medical emergencies and first aid care for the horse; and injury assessment and first aid care for humans. Some courses include helpful photographs that illustrate life-saving techniques, PDF files for writing your plan, and supply checklists for your emergency preparedness kits.

Plan a staff meeting (see box on the right) to work through your farm's emergency preparedness plans for accidents as well as disasters such as floods, tornadoes, fires, and other unpredictable situations. The American Association of Equine Practitioners (AAEP) is an excellent resource: look for it on the Internet. See chapter 4, Riding Programs, Boarding, and Leasing, for more information.

Staff Safety Procedures

Have a staff meeting and talk to your instructors about what to do in case of an emergency. Depending on the incident, these procedures might include the following — all of which might need to happen simultaneously:

1. Stay calm.

2. Designate someone to call 911 (if needed), the camp director, and parents.

3. Designate someone to secure any loose horses.

4. Designate someone to fill out an incident report detailing the accident, treatment given, parents called, horse involved, etc. Have a file or notebook readily available and earmarked for this purpose.

Ahead of time, everyone should know the location of first-aid kits for horses and riders, parents' emergency contact information and release forms, and the "incident report" notebook.

Camp Curriculum

Develop a curriculum for each level of camper and, at the end of each camp session, award certificates of merit to each camper for mastering the lessons. The basic curriculum levels could be beginner, intermediate, and advanced; you could even devise a "Grand Prix level" if you wish.

Examples of curricula for the first three levels appear on the next page. You can change them or combine them as you deem appropriate for your campers and teaching plans.

BEGINNER-LEVEL CURRICULUM GOALS

Campers will learn:

- The parts of the saddle
- The parts of the bridle
- Five major parts of the horse
- Three riding aids
- Basic grooming equipment used on a horse
- The five basic coat colors
- How to tell when a horse is adequately "cooled out"

Campers will be able to demonstrate:

- The proper way to approach a stabled horse
- How to groom and tack up, including picking up and cleaning hooves
- The correct way to lead a horse
- Mounting and dismounting techniques
- Walking, posting trot, and halting
- Riding a figure eight
- Mucking out a stall
- Haltering and unhaltering
- Properly turning out a horse

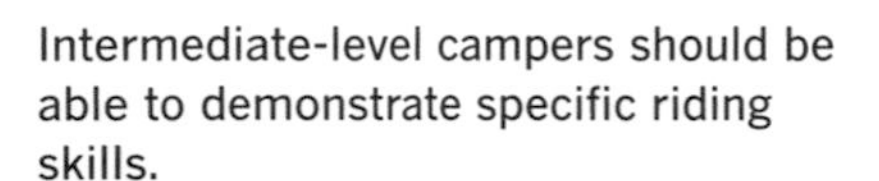

Intermediate-level campers should be able to demonstrate specific riding skills.

INTERMEDIATE-LEVEL CURRICULUM GOALS

Campers will learn:

- The basic differences between good and poor conformation
- Basic horse rations
- Annual inoculations that horses must have
- How to take a horse's temperature
- The differences among a stallion, gelding, mare, colt, filly, and foal
- Two major parasites affecting horses and how to prevent and treat them
- The step sequence for the walk, trot, canter, and gallop
- Cross-cantering and counter-cantering
- The aids used to ask a horse for the right and left leads

Campers will be able to demonstrate:

- Bathing a horse
- Pulling a mane
- Disassembling, cleaning, and reassembling a saddle and bridle
- First aid for minor horse cuts

- Taking a horse's temperature
- How to braid a mane
- How to give and accept a leg up
- How to jump a 2-foot course of fences
- Riding a figure eight and a serpentine
- Posting on the correct diagonal and cantering on the correct lead
- Riding safely on the trail
- Posting to the trot without stirrups
- Blanketing and unblanketing a horse

ADVANCED-LEVEL CURRICULUM GOALS

Campers will learn:

- Ten parts of the horse's musculoskeletal system
- About floating teeth
- The gestation period of a mare
- How many teeth male and female horses have
- The age at which a junior rider loses junior status
- How many hands high is a small, medium, and large pony
- Four color breeds
- The official birthday of Thoroughbreds
- To identify a splint, a wind puff, and a bowel tendon
- The initial treatment for colic
- The amount of water horses require daily

Campers will be able to demonstrate:

- Braiding a tail
- Fitting a bridle and saddle
- Treatment for thrush
- Treatment for abscesses
- Longeing a horse
- How to prepare a bran mash
- Riding a 3-foot course of fences
- Riding a cross-country course with 2-foot jumps
- Simple and flying lead changes
- Turning on the forehand
- Jumping without stirrups

Learning the Lingo

On the next pages are drawings you can photocopy to help your students learn the parts of a saddle and the anatomy of a horse.

Make sure to include opportunities for campers and horses to relax and refresh themselves throughout the day.

Identify the parts of an English saddle

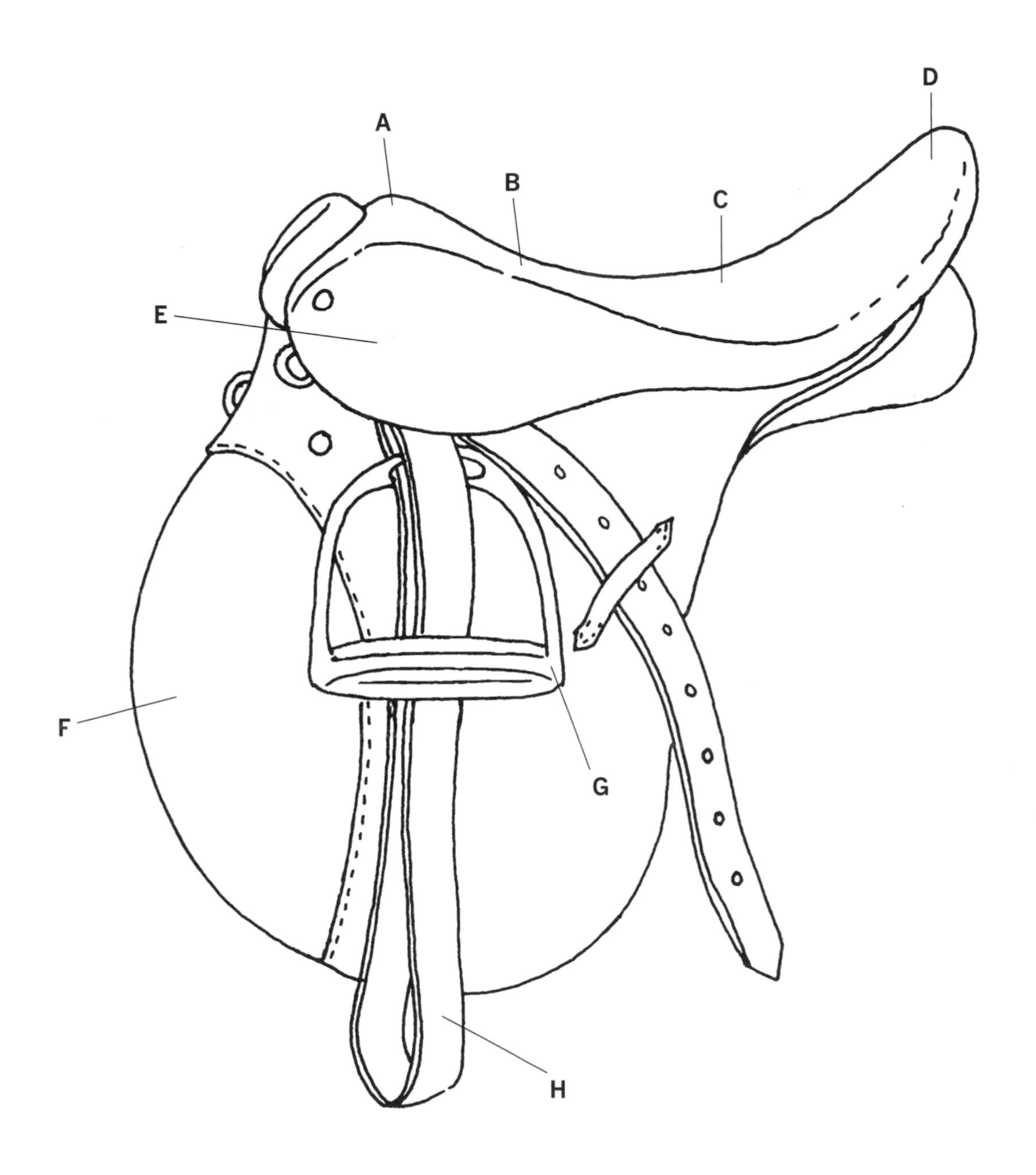

A–pommel, B–waist, C–seat, D–cantle, E–skirt, F–flap, G–stirrup iron, H–stirrup leather

Identify the parts of a Western saddle

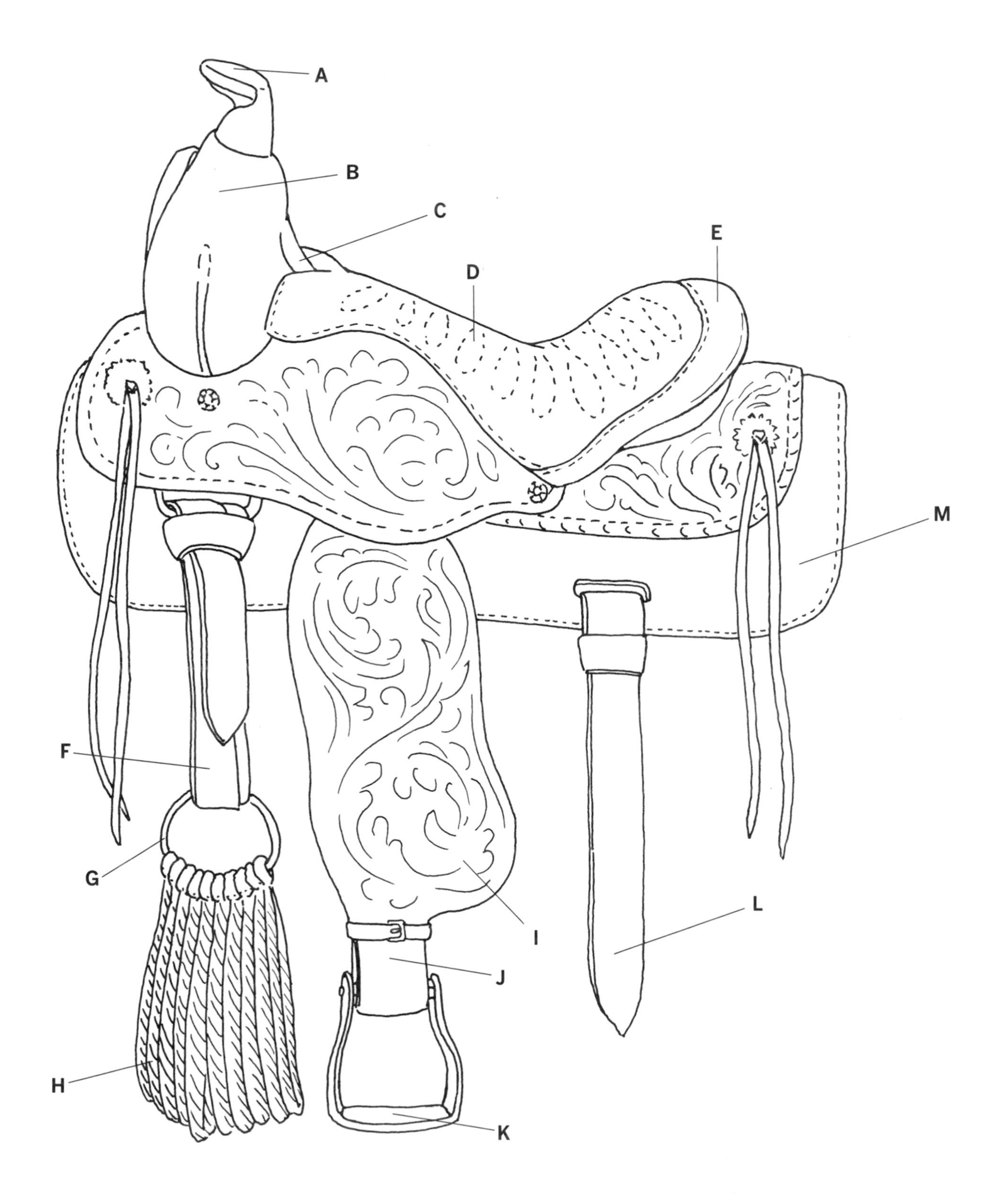

A–horn, B–pommel, C–fork, D–seat, E–cantle, F–latigo, G–cinch ring, H–girth, I–fender, J–stirrup leather, K–stirrup, L–flank billet, M–skirt

Identify the parts of a horse

A–crest, B–poll, C–forehead, D–muzzle, E–throatlatch, F–shoulder, G–knee, H–hoof, I–pastern, J–fetlock, K–cannon bone, L–chestnut, M–coronary band or coronet, N–hock, O–stifle, P–flank, Q–dock, R–back, S–withers

Typical Camp Day

Each hour of every camp day should be planned ahead of time. The last thing you want is a group of campers standing around wondering what to do and later telling their parents they were bored. Specific activities should vary from day to day. Make sure the basic daily schedule is flexible, too, to accommodate special activities such as field trips.

An example of a typical camp day follows:

9:00 A.M. Review events of the day and explain or reiterate safety rules. Students get a short lesson based on the curriculum for their level. Students groom and tack up, with assistance from instructors as necessary.

10:15 A.M. Mounted hour-long lesson, starting with mounted stretching exercises.

11:15 A.M. Students cool down horses, sponge if necessary, groom, and put away tack.

Noon. Lunch break/games.

1:00 P.M. Listen to a ground lecture and watch a demonstration on subjects such as grooming for show or horse health. Consider asking your farrier or veterinarian to come one day and give a guest lecture during this time.

2:00 P.M. Students groom again and tack up.

2:30 P.M. Trail ride or mounted games and activities (see ideas below).

3:30 P.M. Students cool down horses, groom, put away tack, and gather their belongings to leave at 4:00 P.M.

Field Trip!

Ride in the morning, then spend the afternoon taking campers to visit another type of horse operation. You could visit a farm with a completely different purpose from yours, your local equine rescue league, or an equine veterinary hospital. Arrange ahead of time for someone at the destination to give your campers a tour.

First, however, check that your insurance will cover you if any mishaps occur while transporting campers. Make sure the parents know that the campers are traveling off your premises and have them sign a permission form for that date.

Games and Activities

You'll want to have two lengthy lists of games and activities. One will be for activities on the ground and another for those played while mounted.

Campers can be divided into teams for some games and, at the end of a camp session, each participant on the team with the most points receives a prize, such as gift certificate for a few dollars to the tack shop or a small meal at the local fast-food restaurant. There should be no losers, of course, so give members of the other teams a prize, too. A description of some games follows. Select the ones that are appropriate for the age and ability of your campers.

Make a Proclamation

Offer a certificate of merit for campers' achievements. A sample certificate appears in appendix F on page 201.

The United States Pony Club has a list of games on its Web site complete with rules and diagrams. There is every game you can imagine from "Housewife Scurry" to "Postman's Chase" — just do an online search for "Pony Club Games."

GROUND GAMES

Horse Sense. Players are blindfolded, then try to identify certain parts of a very docile, live horse.

Carrot Bobbing. A carrot on a string is tied to each camper's waist and left dangling about 1 foot (0.30 m) from the seat of his or her britches. Each camper has to squat and try to get the carrot into a small coffee can on the ground. Campers can then feed the carrots to the horses.

Scavenger Hunt. Camp teams are each given a list of items they must find around the farm. The items might include a four-leaf clover, an oat kernel, a horse shoe, and a bell boot. The first team to come back with all the items wins.

Tack Test. Each player or team is given a bridle. At a signal, they take it completely apart. The first one to put it back together correctly wins.

Horse Bowl. Players are divided into two groups. Various equine-related questions are asked. The team that answers the most questions correctly wins. Consider the age and level of ability of your campers when creating the questions. The questions can be presented in written form or asked by an instructor much the way quiz games are set up. If the first team misses the question, the other team gets a chance to answer. Whichever team answers the most questions correctly is the winner. The 4-H program has state and national competitions for the Horse Bowl where interested campers may be able to compete.

Boot Race. This is a fun foot race where all the students remove their boots or shoes and put them in a big pile, scrambling them all together. Then, they divide into teams and do a relay race to the pile. Each student must run down sock-footed, put their boots on, and gallop back to tag the next student in line. The first team to "be shod" wins!

Balloon Pop. Everyone gets a balloon; the first one to blow it up, tie it shut, sit on it, and pop it wins! A variation can be played with water balloons — a refreshing treat for campers on a very hot day. To play, two lines are formed, about 1 yard (1 m) apart. Players directly opposite each other are partners. The players in one line toss their balloons to their partners in the other line, and everyone takes one step back after each toss. Continue until there is only one set of children left with an unbroken balloon. These are the winners. The same game can be played with eggs.

SCOTTISH HIGHLAND AND RENAISSANCE GAMES

Most students enjoy dressing up in period costumes, and Scottish Highland and Renaissance games are fun themes to try. Tossing a big log for a caber (definition: a young tree trunk tossed as a trial of strength in a Scottish sport), playing tug of war with a long rope across a creek, doing the sheep toss (bags of hay thrown with a pitchfork), tossing rocks, jousting, and pole bending all make for a fun day. Check online for games and costumes that might be appropriate for your students.

Warn your counselors and instructors to be alert — and patient — at all times.

We had a really fun Highland Games at our farm. Both teams used colorful face paint as shown in the film *Braveheart.* My husband gave a brief history of Scottish clans and feuds, and a local bagpipe player (dressed in his kilt) made the competition between the two teams, the McDonalds and the Campbells, feel truly authentic!

MOUNTED GAMES

Flour and Dime Race. Riders from each team race up to a pie pan filled with flour. They leap off their ponies and blow the flour out of the pan until they reach a dime at the bottom. They hop back onto their mounts and race to the finish line. The first team whose players all finish is the winner. (Make sure none of your riders suffer from asthma.)

Egg Race. One at a time, team riders carry a raw egg on a spoon the length of the riding ring, at a walk. The team that gets the most whole eggs to the other side wins. For older children, you might require them to trot. This game can also be played with potatoes.

The exciting egg race — with raw eggs — tests eye and hand coordination and one-handed riding ability.

Horse Costume Day. Campers bring items from home to dress up their favorite horse. After a parade, counselors or the campers vote to select the best costume. Add different categories so lots of kids win. Take pictures to send home with the camper at the end of the session.

Equestrian Event Day. Campers organize and perform their own equestrian event.

Mock Fox Hunt. (See chapter 6 for complete details.)

Dressage Mini-Show and Tea Party. Map out a dressage test ahead of time. Start off the event with a short lecture on the history of dressage. Campers then mount their horses and each performs the same, small portion of the dressage test as you talk him or her through. Have counselors judge the contestants. Give the winner a blue ribbon and award red ribbons to all other participants. Follow with a bona fide tea party. (See page 103 for a menu.)

Sometimes running a summer camp can be a zoo! Even your counselors and instructors can get into the act on Costume Day.

Parents' Day

One of the best ways to show parents what they received for their money is to invite them to their child's last afternoon at camp. This is when children can show their family and friends all that they have learned and how much fun camp has been.

Plan the show carefully. Start out with the more formal events, when you will want campers to look neat and tidy, then move on to the more boisterous activities. The events of the afternoon might go in this order:

- Campers groom horses appropriately for show — braiding manes, polishing hooves, and so on — just before parents arrive.
- Walk/trot class
- Command class
- Favorite mounted game, such as the egg race
- Horse costume parade
- Award team prizes
- Serve snacks and refreshments to parents while campers untack, groom, and put horses in stalls.

Chances are that parents will sign up their children for camp next year. If your camp proves to be a financial success and you have the facilities, consider offering an overnight camp and earn an even greater profit. Don't forget to do a partial budget as explained in chapter 3 to ensure that an overnight camp will be profitable.

Holiday Celebrations

Here are just a few of the holidays you can celebrate on horseback.

Thanksgiving. Dress up as Pilgrims and Indians and play "Capture the Flag"!

Christmas. Have a live Nativity scene. Don't have any sheep? That little white Shetland pony can be dressed up as a sheep; the black horses can be the cattle lowing the Baby Jesus to sleep. Pipe in some Christmas music and have some eggnog and wassail. Be creative!

Valentine's Day. Dress up your quieter horses as living "Valentine's cards" and give a prize for the best costume.

Easter. Have a mounted Easter egg hunt. Use the Resurrection eggs (look online to order) and chocolate eggs as well. Can your students pick up eggs from horseback?

It's important to end the week with a demonstration of what your campers have learned.

MONEY-MAKING EVENTS AND IDEAS

Many horse operations already conduct money-making programs, such as camps, which are major endeavors. They could increase profits by supplementing those programs with short-term events that bring in money and promote the business but require less planning and personnel. This chapter is chock full of ideas to help you toward this end.

Make sure your events are well organized and runs smoothly, but don't forget the fun. For example, if people have a good time at your show (enjoying the ribbons and prizes, food, and location) then they will come back to the next one.

Look for ways to make events extra enjoyable. A funny, relaxed announcer, for example, can really set a great mood, and people enjoy the day and come back year after year. We need to remember that horse shows are supposed to be recreational and refreshing!

Horse Shows

You may think that putting on a horse show is beyond your abilities; however, provided you have the facilities and the personnel, running such an event can be both profitable and enjoyable.

First, consider the participants for the show. What is your target audience? Do you have many beginners, intermediate students, or even advanced students? What are their needs? Will you conduct a schooling show or a rated show? If, for example, you have a large number of green horses that need mileage, you should have a schooling horse show. Whatever show you decide to have, remember to keep the atmosphere relaxed and fun.

It is essential to check with local riding associations to make sure your date does not conflict with any show they are having. Finding a clear date can be difficult, but it will pay off in the long run. Most riders that join riding associations are doing it for points and will not take the chance of missing one of their shows to attend yours.

SHOW PLANNING: A MULTITUDE OF DETAILS

There are dozens of details to keep in mind as you plan and execute a horse show. Here are some things to think about from the beginning. Since all have to be considered simultaneously, I list them alphabetically, not chronologically.

Concessions

It is always nice to have a concession stand where the participants can get drinks, lunch, and snacks. You can almost always find a local 4-H club to do this, but other groups may be interested, too. Check with your local school's PTA or PTO, arts groups, sports teams, or church youth groups.

If you want something more up-scale, contact a local restaurant to see if it is interested in catering. Our local barbecue restaurant will bring everything for a nice full meal without charging us; instead they receive all of the profits. The smell of smoked BBQ wafting through the show area adds to the festive ambience.

Donations

To save money putting on a show, try using as many donations and volunteers as you can — judge, ring, concessions, and so on. See if you can arrange things so that the ribbons are the only item you pay for.

Be sure to thank your volunteers and donors publicly, both during and after the event.

Don't Overprice Yourself

Entry fees should be competitive with comparable shows in the area; otherwise, riders just might forgo your show to ride in the less costly ones.

Emergency Personnel

Invite the local rescue squad to attend or at least let them know you are having a show, when, and where. A nice donation will make them happy to be there, which is important for safety reasons. Some horse shows charge an EMT fee that can run from $5 to $20 and more per rider.

Entry Fees

It currently costs about $15 to enter a class in a small local show, and some places will charge $35 to $40 for a division of three classes. Bigger shows have bigger price tags. A friend of mine says she budgets a little over $1,000 for an A show. This includes a night or two in a hotel, braiding, ground fees, stall fees, entry fees, food, and incidentals.

Insurance

Insurance is a must and can be quite pricey. In our area the smaller riding clubs are required to carry a $1 million policy for each show. Consult with your insurance carrier for information.

Judges

It costs $300 and up to hire a judge, unless you can persuade a former 4-H or Pony Club member to do it for free.

Parking

Make sure there is adequate parking for cars and trailers, with clear signage. Have a tractor available to pull out stuck vehicles if it rains.

Photography

Locate a photographer who can take pictures at the show. Parents love photographs of their children showing, and teens and adults love pictures of themselves and their horses doing what they do best. The photographer should have a Web site or a portable printer where he or she can sell pictures. Offer them a free spot, or charge $10 to $25. In this economy, they may jump at the chance to have a "captive audience" of prospective clients.

Clear signage makes a smoothly flowing show day.

Post-Show Publicity

After the show, be sure to send an article to the local paper naming the champions, and include some pictures if possible. See if you can get your photographer to donate a good picture. Don't forget to give him or her a credit line for the photo in the paper.

This is a good way to get free advertising for your next show. Remember to mention it in your press release.

Prizes, Ribbons, and Trophies

Ribbons and trophies must be of good quality, but affordable. Catherine Akins, a 4-H leader in Powhatan, Virginia, who has organized many shows, adds this recommendation:

"Hodges Badge Company has a great horse show planning book they send you when you order ribbons from them. They also have a wonderful package deal called 'show in a box' which includes nice ribbons and a box of everything you need for a show from numbers and strings to pencils, duct tape, and toilet paper! It cost around $600 for everything for our last show, which had 24 classes. The package included ribbons (first through sixth place), with our club name printed on them, and trophies for division championships. They also sent brushes, stationery packets, and little things like that. Best of all, everything arrived in a very timely manner."

Ask local tack shops or feed stores for donations of prizes and then you will need to order only the ribbons.

Rings

If you don't have a ring, it can be pricey to rent one. They can range from free to several hundreds of dollars depending on what the facility offers. 4-H clubs usually have them donated. Call the facilities you are interested in to ask their price and see if they will negotiate.

Tack Sales

Check around your area and see if there is a tack shop that would like to set up a tent and bring tack to sell. Ask for a percentage of the sales, or offer a "spot" as with the photographer.

Spread the Word

Send out a lot of flyers, run notices in the papers, put up posters, and tell everyone you know.

Many people e-mail or snail-mail their show schedule and prize list to all the barns and local riding clubs in the area. You can also ask local 4-H extension leaders to send out a mass e-mail to all the horse clubs and 4-Hers in the area.

After you've run a show once or twice, it becomes easier. If your event is fun and well run, people will want to come back for the next one.

Costs of a Small Show

If you have volunteers and and the facilities, jumps, and equipment on your farm, you can probably run a small show for around $1,000 to $1,500. Here are some rough guidelines:

Judge $300

Ribbons $600

Donation to supplier of PA system $100–200

Donation to EMT $100–200

Let your riders show their creativity in a costume class.

Water

Access to fresh water is essential, both for the horses to drink and for bathing them.

SCHOOLING/OPEN SHOWS

Schooling/open shows are good confidence builders for riders and horses, and often spur them on to better performances. They also expose parents and grandparents to the horse world. Often, proud parents, seeing their children show a horse, will sign them up for additional lessons. They may even lease or purchase a horse.

Show Class Ideas

- **School horses only.** This class is open to all horses used by riding schools for teaching lessons.
- **Lead-line.** Students must be under 6 years old.
- **Golden oldies.** Entrants must be more than 45 years old.
- **Baby or pregreen.** These are schooling classes for horses in their first 6 months of showing.
- **Dollar bill.** Each rider holds a dollar bill under one knee at the walk, trot, and canter. Whoever keeps it there the longest wins. No chaps or shorts allowed!
- **Pairs.** Two riders are judged at the walk, trot, and canter as they ride almost knee to knee.
- **Costume.** Riders dress themselves and their horses in costumes of their choice or according to a theme. They are judged on creativity and originality.
- **Local hunter.** This class is open to horses stabled within 50 miles of the show grounds.
- **Short stirrup.** Only riders under the age of 10 are eligible.

HORSE SHOW ASSOCIATIONS

If the competitive level of your target audience is somewhere between a schooling show and a rated show, you may want to join or form a local association that organizes several horse shows every year. Points won at each show are added up at year's end, and the leaders are the champions of your horse-show association. You could also sponsor a year-end awards banquet to honor winners and raise money for a local veterinary school or equine rescue league.

RATED SHOWS

If you determine that you have a more advanced target audience consisting of students and horses that are more competitive and need points, you can have a rated show. Contact the United States Equestrian Federation for further information (see appendix L, page 217, for contact information).

SHOW PLANNING CALENDAR

Managing a horse show takes a lot of organization and delegation. For your first show, especially, it's worth the money to get quality jumps, ribbons, trophies, and a good judge. Your extra effort will give you a good reputation and bring more participants to future shows. If you make the schooling shows open to riders from other farms, you never know — some of them just might decide to stay.

Six to twelve months before the show:

- Book the judge, decide on the classes, and print the program flyer, including the prize list. (Include a horse-show checklist; it can be sent as a gift with the prize list. See the example on page 99.) Ask one or two local vendors, including tack and feed stores, to advertise in the flyer to offset the cost of promoting the show. The cover of the prize list should include the location, date, time, judge, and a rain date of the show.
- The inside of the program flyer should include the list of classes, entry fees for each class, and rules, including prizes to be awarded.

Three to six months in advance:

- Order the ribbons, exhibitors' numbers, and judge's cards.
- Secure the announcer, judge, show secretary, course designer, jump crew, runners, and gateman (call to confirm 2 weeks before the show). Make sure they are also available for the rain date.
- Organize a concession stand and arrange for personnel.
- Obtain a public address system or megaphones. The local rescue squad or public school may lend you a PA system or try to rent one from a rental outfit.

Sample: Safety Rules and Regulations

- All riders entering the arena acknowledge and accept that they are riding at their own risk.
- All riders under the age of 16 must be accompanied by a parent or guardian who assumes full responsibility for the conduct and safety of the child while attending any event or activities.
- All riders are required to wear ASTM/SEI safety helmets at club-sanctioned events while they are mounted or when working with the horses.
- Riders should use the main entrance of the building.
- Respect the arena property and the property of others. Any breakages must be paid for. Please leave the arena as you find it.
- Practice good horsemanship and good conduct.
- Ensure that your horse is properly secured in the appropriate areas.
- Ensure that all manure from arena is picked up and put in designated area.
- Abusive behavior toward a horse will not be tolerated at anytime for any reason.
- No alcoholic beverages on premises.

Establishing Rules for Your Show

In your program you can set forth guidelines and rules for the show. These might include, for example, that all horses must come with evidence of a current negative Coggins test, dogs must be leashed at all times, riders must wear hard hats while mounted, and the farm and its employees are not responsible for any accident, injury, or loss occurring during the show.

You might also explain that a trophy and six ribbons will be awarded in all classes, and a championship trophy and ribbon and reserve championship ribbon will be awarded in the following divisions (then list according to classes planned).

One month in advance:

- Rent several portable toilets, if necessary, and buy sufficient toilet paper.
- Secure adequate trash receptacles and arrange for them to be emptied.
- Have equipment, such as jumps, painted as needed.
- Ask local emergency medical personnel to be on hand for the show. If the show is large enough to disrupt traffic, alert police.

The day before the show:

- Pray for good weather and a good turnout (but remember, you planned a rain date).
- Disk and drag rings.
- Get change for the cash box.
- Mow grass.
- Set up the first course.
- Put up signs and directional arrows since riders and the judge will start showing up early the next day.
- Clearly mark parking area, portable toilets or rest rooms, water faucets, entry booth, and so on.
- Organize ribbons and trophies for each class.
- Try to get some rest the day before the show: you will need it.

The day of the show:

- Be sure to check each horse for negative Coggins test.
- Provide clipboard, judge's cards, and pencils for the judge.
- Provide the judge with food and drink.
- Post course designs for classes.
- Make sure the jump crew knows when to change fences and to what height.
- Recheck all points before awarding championships.
- Keep the show moving along.
- Post judge's cards.
- Pay the judge, announcer, and other assistants.

Horse Show Checklist

Distribute this checklist to all of your horse-show participants when you send out the prize list. Include your farm logo, and they'll always remember you (when they pull it out for other shows).

Horse Supplies

- ☐ Coggins test results
- ☐ Membership card
- ☐ Saddle
- ☐ Pad
- ☐ Girth
- ☐ Bridle
- ☐ Martingale
- ☐ Halter
- ☐ Extra bits
- ☐ Splint boots
- ☐ Bell boots
- ☐ Lead line
- ☐ Crop
- ☐ Hay and hay net
- ☐ Buckets
- ☐ Extra reins
- ☐ Body brush
- ☐ Dandy brush
- ☐ Finishing brush
- ☐ Hoof pick
- ☐ Mane comb
- ☐ Sweat scraper
- ☐ Curry comb
- ☐ Fly spray
- ☐ Braiding kit
- ☐ Rubber bands
- ☐ Yarn
- ☐ Scissors
- ☐ Coat polish
- ☐ Hoof dressing
- ☐ Shampoo
- ☐ Baby powder
- ☐ Vaseline
- ☐ Baby wipes
- ☐ First-aid kit

Rider Supplies

- ☐ Hat
- ☐ Coat
- ☐ Ratcatcher and collar
- ☐ Pants, boots, socks, or knee-highs
- ☐ Collar pin or monogrammed collar
- ☐ Gloves
- ☐ Raincoat and hat cover
- ☐ Spurs
- ☐ Jumping vest
- ☐ Hairnet
- ☐ Rubber boot covers
- ☐ Safety pins, needle, and thread
- ☐ Pain reliever
- ☐ Visor or baseball cap
- ☐ Sunscreen
- ☐ Sunglasses
- ☐ Hand towels
- ☐ First-aid kit

The day after the show:

- Make sure all trash is collected.
- Return all rented equipment.
- Tally up all the receipts and cash, and make deposits and pay bills pertaining to expenses. (I worked for a couple once who went to Las Vegas after every horse show. They never did deposit any money in the bank. I don't recommend this.)

Create an Instant Display

Scrapbooks and photo albums are great ways to exhibit all that your farm has to offer. Your students may enjoy compiling and updating them (although you may need to do a little editing). Display them at any events you host or take them with you to events you attend.

Outline of a Hunter Pace

In a hunter pace, a trail is marked, ahead of time, for a horse and rider to follow. Early in the morning on the day of the competition, an experienced horse and rider set forth to ride the trail as fast as it is safely possible to do so. This morning ride, sometimes called "the dead body run," has two purposes: to ensure that the trail is clear and safe for the competitors, and to establish the "pace time" — the ideal time in which to ride the trail safely.

When the event begins, teams of two or three competitors ride the trail together. At checkpoints along the way, officials ensure that the riders are staying on course and are not overworking their horses.

Each group of riders is timed. Riders are penalized for either riding too fast and beating the pace time, or too slow and taking longer than the pace time. The group to come closest to the pace time wins the competition.

Endurance or Competitive Trail Rides

Hosting an endurance or competitive trail ride can be a great way to get to know others in the area and stimulate interest in the sport. Trail rides vary in length, with a suggested range anywhere between 10 and 100 miles (16–160 km).

On a trail ride, the conditioning and endurance of horse and rider are put to the test. Competitors ride over a predetermined trail. Horses should be closely monitored throughout the ride for soundness and signs of exhaustion, and have their pulse and respiration taken at designated checkpoints. The first horse and rider to cross the finish line, after successfully making it through the checkpoints, win.

To make this a profitable venture, your budget must include an entry fee sufficient to cover the cost of assistants, veterinarians, markers, flyers, mailings, and your time. For more information, contact your local trail-ride association or veterinarian.

Hunter Pace

A fun and profitable alternative to a horse show is a Hunter Pace, a low-key competitive horse event that originated with foxhunting. You can promote this exclusively within your own barn or to the general public. Teams of two or three riders follow an outdoor course laid out over terrain that is meant to simulate the riding conditions encountered during a foxhunt. This would include gaits that a foxhunter uses as a fox's scent is found and followed by hounds through open country, over fences, and along wooded trails.

Brightly colored plastic ribbons mark the course. Participants look for the ribbons, much the way they would have to "listen" for the foxhounds, to know the right direction in which to ride. You can even play prerecorded "hound music" at certain points.

Generally, this requires less equipment and effort on your part than a full-fledged horse show or event. You can set courses for beginning to advanced students.

There is more than one way to organize a Hunter Pace event. One is to come up with a predetermined "optimal time." If you estimate the optimal (not necessarily the fastest)

Beginning to advanced students can compete in a Hunter Pace.

time to ride the course is 30 minutes, whichever rider comes in closest to that time wins. For example, the rider who finishes in 29 minutes wins, not the one who finishes in 28 minutes, because this is not a speed race. You could also award prizes for the fastest and slowest times.

Award ribbons and trophies to the winners. Send press releases to your local papers before and after the event (see chapter 2).

Mock Fox Hunt

The Mock Fox Hunt is an event that all your students, boarders, and those from outside barns can enjoy. This is really just a glorified trail ride with treats and prizes for all participants. The organization of such an event is simple and, with a little imagination, should result in a fun-filled ride for everyone.

PLANNING AHEAD

- Charge a "capping fee," which is the amount of money that hunts usually charge guests who join them. You can charge participants, including your students, an additional fee for the use of your horses.
- Set a date and time.
- Go over the route in advance to eliminate any last-minute surprises.

Fox-Hunting Terminology

The *Master of Foxhounds,* or MFH, is the boss.

The *Huntsman* controls the hounds, and the *Whippers-In* help the Huntsman.

The *Hunt Secretary* collects the capping fee and dues, while the *field* is made up of all the mounted *followers.*

The followers can be divided into a first and a second field. The more advanced riders, who make up the first field, jump the obstacles.

The second field, which is slower, is composed of less experienced riders. They delicately avoid any object that may unsettle their horses or themselves. You might want to invite parents or friends to follow on foot as spectators.

The *brush* is the fox's tail. The *cry* is the sound the fox hounds make while hunting. If you hear someone say the fox *goes to ground,* it means he is hiding, usually underground. The *scent* is the smell of the fox that the hounds follow. *Ware* is an abbreviation for beware, as in "ware wire" or "ware hole."

Brunswick Stew

Traditionally made with squirrel, this classic Virginia hunt country recipe is cooked over an open fire in a cast-iron pot. Today it is usually made with chicken, and vegetarians can even omit the birds if they prefer. You could also cook it in a big pot on the stove.

2 5-pound hens
4 quarts water
7 medium-sized potatoes, diced
4 1-pound cans of lima beans
2 1-pound cans of corn
4 1-pound cans of tomatoes
4 large onions, chopped
1 cup tomato paste
Salt and pepper to taste

Note: Frozen or fresh vegetables can be substituted for canned ones.

1. Cook the chickens in the water for 1 hour. Remove from the cooking pot and debone. Cut up the meat and return to the pot.
2. Add the potatoes, lima beans, corn, tomatoes, onions, tomato paste, and salt and pepper to taste. Cook for 1 hour, stirring occasionally. (Take care not to scorch the bottom of the pot.)

15 to 20 servings

- Organize your "hunt club" and select your "hunt colors." Matching sweatshirts or other clothing is a fun idea and will build camaraderie. You could ask each participant to buy a farm sweatshirt, or include the cost of the shirts in your capping fee.
- It makes the day more interesting for the uninitiated if they have at least a small grasp of hunting terms. Copy the list on page 101 and give it to the mock fox hunters.

CONDUCTING THE EVENT

Designate staff members as the Master of Foxhounds, Huntsman, Whippers-In, and Hunt Secretary. They can wear matching jackets or perhaps pin their titles to their backs to distinguish themselves from the rest of the field.

Design a fox outfit and appoint someone to wear the costume and then hide out at a designated place at the end of the course.

The course can be tracked by actually following the sightings of the "fox" or it can be marked out with riddles leading to the next area of chase. For example, "The fox's tail is colored red, find the next clue behind the shed!" You get the idea.

To add effect, pipe in "hound music" at the clue points. The "hunt" culminates when the fox is found. The fox can then hand out candy or other treats, and everyone returns to the barn.

After the hunt, all participants, including parents and guests who didn't ride, head to the house for Brunswick stew (see the recipe at left) or a big hunt breakfast. Prepare the meal ahead of time and charge guests a fee, or everyone can provide the ingredients.

This social event gives your barn great exposure and creates good public relations with the parents who pay the bills. It is also a noncompetitive event; the pleasure riders at your barn who do not participate in other horse events can join in this good time.

Hayrides

Hayrides are another fun and profitable venture. Use the ideas in chapter 2 to promote them. If people have a good time and are interested in horses, perhaps they'll be interested in hearing about other events and services you offer.

As with trail rides, you can bring in more hayriders by offering discount rates to groups.

Dressage Show and Tea Party

Consider a dressage show for students and boarders. Open it up to those from other farms if you want, and invite parents, siblings, and grandparents to watch the show and attend the party. Riding contestants can be judged by your own qualified instructors or by guest judges.

Afterward, have an authentic British tea party. Charge enough per contestant and guest to cover your costs and make a profit.

Contests

Photo, video, literary, art, horse-bowl, and horse-judging contests are all great ways to stimulate interest in your barn.

Photo contests require entrants to submit photos they have taken themselves of their own horses or the stable horses. Contestants choose the captions. Post the winners on your bulletin board in full view for visitors to see.

Videos and DVDs, a maximum of 15 minutes long, can be educational or amusing. Offer prizes for the best horse-safety video, horses at play, before and after a year's worth of riding lessons, or how *not* to clean a stall.

Literary contestants submit either a poem or an essay (1,500 words or less) on a horse-related topic; it can be serious, such as the proper way to treat a colicky horse, or fun, such as why your horse is your best friend in 100 words or less.

Judge art contestants on their creativity and the overall appearance of their work. Display entries in the office.

Organize horse-bowl competitions to test knowledge of horse-related topics. This is a fast-paced game of recall complete with buzzers. Four players on each team sound a buzzer and must correctly answer the questions before the other team does.

Dressage Tea Party Menu

Earl Grey tea, iced and hot

Quiche (any kind you like)

Deviled eggs

Scones with clotted cream and lemon curd

Shortbread

Fruit cake

Cucumber sandwiches

To make: Cut crusts off white bread, lightly butter, fill with sliced cucumbers, then cut sandwiches into quarters. Children will enjoy these sandwiches even more if you use cookie cutters to cut them into the shape of a horse, horse head, heart, or circle.

Horse-judging contests consist of several classes of horses brought out and evaluated by contestants. A qualified instructor should make the official placing. After the contestants have judged the classes, they must defend their rationale for placing classes in a certain order. This is known as giving "oral reasons." Contestants who place the class correctly and give good oral reasons for their decisions are the winners.

Require a small entry fee for each contest. Distribute ribbons, trophies, tack, a free lesson, or cash awards to the winners. Make sure you charge enough to make a profit, covering both your expenses and your time.

Breed Trail Rides

Perhaps you would like to get your riders involved in a breed-organization trail ride, such as ones conducted by the American Quarter Horse Association. Or you could start your own trail ride award system and offer prizes for those riders who ride the most throughout the year. See the Virginia Quarter Horse Riding Program in appendix L.

Public Trail Rides

Offering trail rides can be a great financial opportunity. This is true particularly if they bring in long-term customers.

The first and last exposure to riding many people have is renting a trail horse by the hour. Be sure to make the experience as enjoyable as possible by providing clients with well-behaved horses. Have an experienced instructor or rider lead the ride at a pace appropriate for the group's level of experience. Give a quick lesson on how to get a horse to go and stop, even for those riders who say they have ridden horses before. On the trail, if a rider is having trouble with a horse, take the time to find out why and, if necessary, swap horses with the rider.

Since trail riding may be the only contact the public has with horses, make it a winning experience.

For longer trail rides, don't be afraid to be creative. A stable in Virginia offers romantic trail rides. They guide riders to a secluded moonlit spot, provide a picnic, and let them wander back to the barn at their leisure. Others offer "cowboy coffee and grub" at the halfway point. You could have a Native American artifact excursion ride, chuck wagon with singing cowboys or sing-alongs, or a Civil War or Revolutionary War ride if you live in an area with historical sites.

This could be a great opportunity for attracting internationals as well. If you live near an area of historical significance, such as a Civil War site, or within a reasonable trailer ride, you can advertise in some of the international horse, history, or travel magazines. First, obtain permission from the park or local landowner, then study the history. Pick out or make up a soldier from that era and dress the part. Take a group on a guided tour of the area explaining the history. Perhaps if you are near Appomattox, you could even do it from the perspective of "Traveler" (Robert E. Lee's horse).

Share some local history tidbit not found in the guidebooks to keep it interesting. End the trail ride with a historical country lunch, perhaps Smithfield ham on buttered biscuits and apple cider.

Attract trail riders by offering discount rates to church groups, civic organizations, and schools.

After taking a group out on a trail ride, offer your farm brochure and event calendar to the riders. Let them know that you offer riding lessons.

Vending Machines

They may have little to do with horses directly, but providing vending machines with drinks is a service to visitors and will generate a small income for you. The drink companies supply the machines, deliver the drinks, and do all the maintenance and repairs.

Depending on your selling price and the profit margin in your area, you can earn $0.15–$0.30 on each drink. If you sell 20 drinks every day and earn $0.20 per drink, you will have increased your profits by over $1,460 at the end of the year.

Offer some healthy fruit drinks and water as well as soft drinks. If you have many parents waiting to pick up their children from lessons, coffee and tea can be in demand.

A snack machine can also increase your profits; just make sure the students dispose of their trash properly. Make sure to check with parents if their children have disabilities or special diets, like peanut allergies, to be on the safe side.

Use the drink machine to add more fun to your school by requiring students who fall off their horses to buy their instructor a soda!

Fall Harvest Days

One of my dairy-farmer clients found that it was more profitable to use his farm for a fall harvest days celebration than to produce milk. He plants acres of corn and pumpkins. In fall, he cuts mazes in the cornfield so that kids can start at one end and hopefully find their way out the other end. He also takes hayrides out to the pumpkin field where visitors can pick their own pumpkins.

The milking parlor is set up with old Bessie, where city kids can pet and milk a cow before heading back to the barn for kettle corn and smoked BBQ. Large bins hold apples for

Educational Activities

Offer events such as short courses, seminars, and clinics to advertise your business, generate revenue, and educate you and your students. Try to bring in a well-known, reputable judge or horse trainer; she'll add credibility to the event and draw more participants.

sale, as well as stalks of corn for decorating. An area is designated for local crafters to sell their wares as well.

Perhaps there is an area on your farm where you could offer some of these activities to increase your profits in fall.

Retirees, Rescue Horses, and End-of-Life Care for Equines

The United States has closed all equine slaughter facilities in this country. Whether or not you agree with this legislation, the fact is that now there is a huge population of unwanted horses with no place to go. At livestock markets, you can sometimes find horses with a sign around their necks saying *"free!"* Recently, I was told by one of my clients that he had hauled some horses down to Texas from Virginia, and on the return trip he stayed in a hotel. The next morning when he came out, someone had left four horses in his trailer!

This surplus of unwanted horses may open up some new possibilities in the horse business.

Think creatively about your farm's possibilities. What about opening an equine assisted-living facility or an equine cemetery?

RETIREMENT BOARDING

If your farm is in the country, it is likely that the cost of operating a boarding facility is less than in the city. Many people would like to keep their retired horse safe and comfortable until it reaches the end of his life; however, the cost can be prohibitive if they live in or near a city. Board could be $500 per month in the city, whereas you could offer it for $300 and still make a good profit. You can advertise as "a retirement community with assisted living" for the older horse, maybe with Cushing's disease, which needs daily medication. For an additional charge, you take care of grooming and foot trimming as well as health care. Advertise in the city newspapers and see whether you get some clients.

EQUINE CEMETERY OR CREMATORIUM

If you have the land and no problems with water flow or county restrictions, you may be able to open an equine cemetery. Check with your local government to make sure no restrictions apply. A crematorium could also be a possibility, where you can return the ashes of the horse in a nice urn to the owner.

Perhaps you can become one of the facilities that take unwanted horses. The Association of American Equine Practitioners has set guidelines for acceptable health care for unwanted horses, which must be followed. Check online for more information on how to get involved and the possibility of taking some unwanted horses. (See appendix L.)

This could be a money-making opportunity for you as well as a good service to the horse industry. Be sure, however, that all of your costs are covered and someone is paying for the life of the horse. Otherwise, you could get stuck with many unwanted horses and lose money as well. If it is not financially sustainable, it does not help you or the horses in the long run.

Unwanted Horse Coalition

The mission of the Unwanted Horse Coalition is to reduce the number of unwanted horses and to improve their welfare through education and the efforts of organizations committed to the health, safety, and responsible care and disposition of these horses.

The Unwanted Horse Coalition, a broad alliance of equine organizations that have joined together under the American Horse Council, is concerned that some horses may slip through the various safety nets within the equine industry. Too many owners are unaware of, or do not give enough thought to, the available options, services, and assistance available in the industry to help them ensure that their horse has caring and humane support throughout his life. The Unwanted Horse Coalition will help educate the horse industry about this issue and help people learn to own responsibly. (See appendix L for contact info.)

Four Secrets of Selling

The secrets to making money on your purchases are:

- Buy low
- Turn over quickly
- Sell for top dollar
- Be a salesperson

will take it to the bank, get the cash back, and give it to the buyer. By the time the check bounces, your horse and all the money are gone.

There are many, many variations of this scam, so do be careful when dealing with people you don't know. Keep your horse until the check clears the bank and *never* send or give the extra money to anyone until you're sure the check is good. This could take 2 or more weeks. The best thing to do is require a certified check from their bank.

In another case, a woman bought a horse from a horse trader. The trader assured the woman he was a fine horse, he just didn't look too good. When she took the horse away from his familiar surroundings, she suspected his eyesight was poor. The veterinarian took a look and told her the horse was practically blind. When the woman tried to return the horse to the horse trader he said, "Ma'am, I told you he didn't look too good." And he refused to refund her money.

Private Contract Sales

The process of buying and selling horses to and from individuals is known as "private contract sales." No matter what kind of horse business you have, buying and selling horses can be a great financial opportunity.

Because there isn't any Blue Book on horses, an animal's value can vary from sale to sale. A horse that may be worth only $750 to you may be worth $2,500 to someone else. Don't be afraid to ask the highest, but still fair, price for your horses.

Buy Low

To buy low, you have to have a good network. Develop contacts at the racetrack and the veterinarian's office. When they come across a buyer who wants to sell a horse quickly, have them call you.

Once I was at the veterinarian's office when someone was trying to sell a horse to another customer. The mare didn't pass the veterinarian's examination because of a severe case of thrush. The owner was so frustrated that she sold me the horse for $500. After a few months of treatment, I sold the mare for $3,000 and made a healthy profit. Sometimes it just takes being in the right place at the right time and a willingness to take some risk.

Turn Over Quickly

Avoid investing too much time and expense on your purchase. To do this, predict how long it will take to get the horse in shape to be sold for a profit. If you have the opportunity to purchase or are given a very thin, malnourished horse, the initial price will be low but, by the time you pay for veterinary bills, shoes, feed, supplements, and training, the total amount of time and money invested in the horse may never be recovered.

Horse people can be eternal optimists, always thinking a particular horse will improve with just a few more training sessions and then it will sell for big bucks. Be realistic. Some horses are just problem horses and will take an eternity to straighten out. Optimism is never warranted with problem horses. In this situation, it is better to bail out early than to invest endlessly. Remember the saying, "Let your profits run long and cut your losses short."

For example, Sue bought a 6-year-old Thoroughbred named Kala off the track, without trying her out, in the hopes of turning her into a show hunter. After a year of training, Kala had progressed very little. When Sue tried to sell the mare for $2,500, many people came to try her out, but only one made an offer of $500. Sue refused to sell at such a loss, so she invested another year's worth of board, veterinary bills, and farrier bills, totaling about $3,500. She would have been wiser to pocket the $500 and save $3,500 in bills.

Sell for Top Dollar

Strive to sell the horse at its peak conditioning, ability, and performance levels. Perception matters. A well-conditioned, well-groomed horse will sell better than a thin horse, even if the less attractive animal is actually a better horse overall. The old horse traders say that the most desirable color for a horse is "fat."

Groom for the Best Impression

A 45-minute clip and clean-up job can make or break the deal and potentially add hundreds of dollars to the sale price.

The Art of Salesmanship

Always say "yes" when negotiating. For example, "Yes, I would like to sell him for that price, but his potential in the show ring makes his value considerably higher," or "Yes, I'll sell him for that price if you trade me the pony you've outgrown." Hold a horse only if you receive a deposit. Allow customers time to think about the purchase, but let them know that you have others who are interested.

Be a Salesperson

Constantly network. Get involved with activities that put you in contact with potential customers. Judge shows; join local, state, or national horse associations; and participate in charity events. Host promotional events (see chapters 2 and 6), and hand out your business cards and a list of horses you are currently selling.

Put up for-sale signs in tack and feed shops and at veterinary clinics. Include a color snapshot or digital image of the horse. Post tear-off tabs of paper with your phone number and "horses for sale" at the bottom.

Before any potential buyers arrive, get organized. Have available all the information on the horses' selling points, such as show or race records, pedigree, pictures, or videos. If the clients are not in the area, mail or e-mail this information to them. When they come, be hospitable.

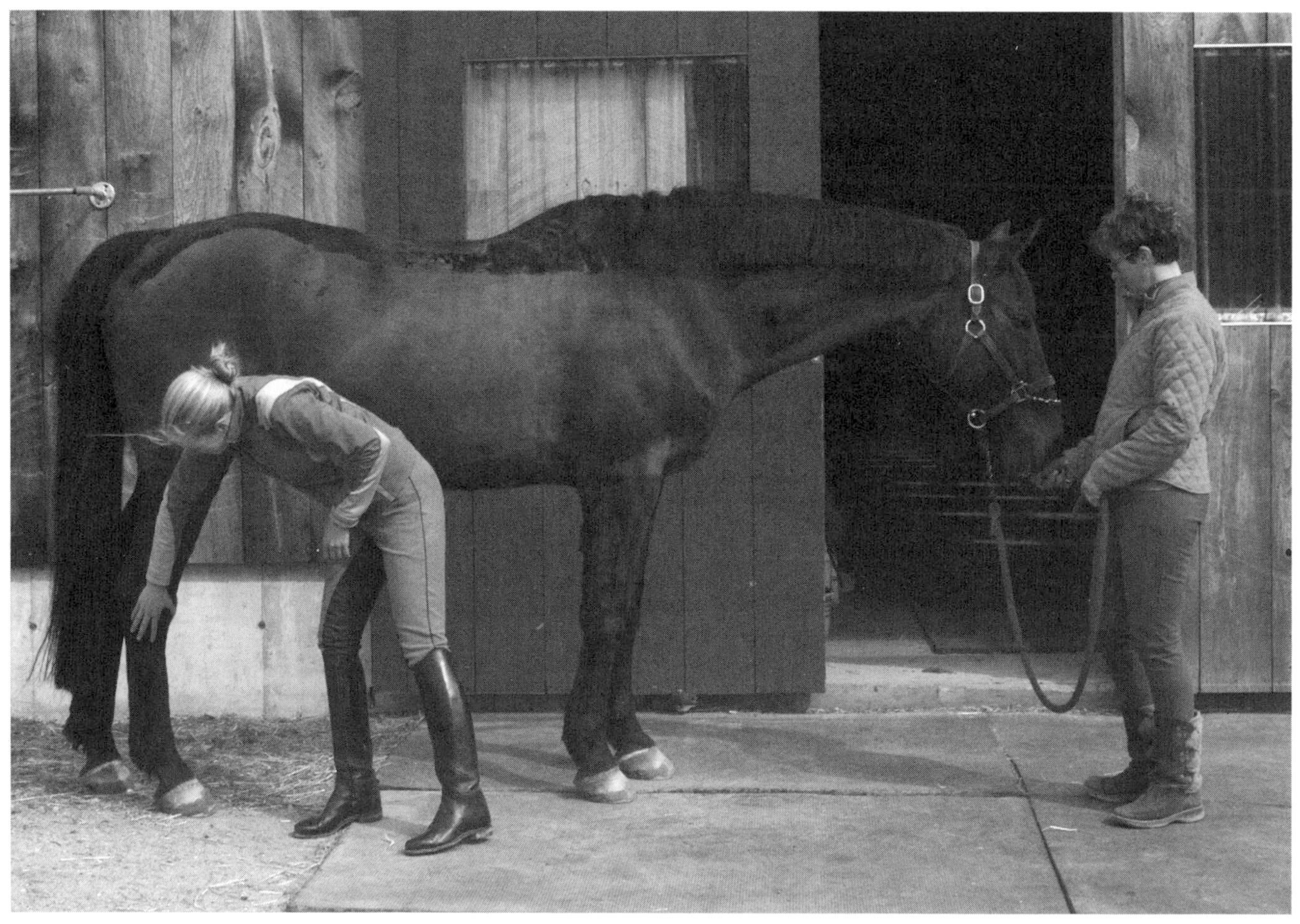

Buying and selling horses can be a great financial opportunity, but avoid investing too much time and expense on your purchase.

MAKING THE DEAL

Take action during the last part of a customer's visit. Promote the horse without being overbearing. This takes finesse and practice. Be honest and direct in stressing all of the horse's good points, but don't lie about his weaknesses if you are asked. Ask about the potential buyer's level of expertise, intended use, and likes and dislikes, and then talk about the horse's strengths, experience, and personality in this context.

For example, by asking questions you learn that the rider is an advanced beginner-to-intermediate rider, would like to have a horse to bring to local shows and enjoy on trail rides, and wants a fairly quiet, dependable mount. So, in talking about the horse for sale, you mention that he has been shown successfully for the past 3 years (mention specific shows and placings if you know them), has been ridden by others, and has excellent manners in the stall and under tack.

Finally, if the customers aren't interested in one horse, keep their names on file and contact them when you find another, more suitable horse for them. Keep them on your mailing list for shows, newsletters, tack sales, and promotional events.

COMMISSIONS

A commission is the fee you receive for performing a certain service. Your time, training, and experience are valuable and shouldn't be given away. When purchasing or selling products for clients, add 10 to 15 percent to the sale price for your commission. This includes selling and buying horses.

When selling a horse for someone, be sure to obtain a written contract that specifies the selling price (the amount desired as well as the lowest acceptable amount), liability issues (who pays if the horse is sick, injured, or killed), the commission you will receive at the time of the sale, and the period of time you have in which to sell the horse.

Let tack shops, trailer suppliers, and other agents know when you refer business to them. Try to work on a commission or arrange for a discount on products you purchase from them.

Learn from My Mistakes

There should be an exclusivity clause that guarantees your commission should any other party sell the horse during the period you are contracted to make the sale. In two instances, I lost commissions. In the first instance, the buyer went around me and purchased the horse directly from my client, who subsequently never paid my commission. In the second instance, I was forced to purchase a horse I had on commission that was badly injured while in the process of being sold. Learn from my mistakes: Be sure to spell out terms and get everything in writing.

Liquidation

An auction also is a way to liquidate your operation if ever the need arises. I once worked at a stable that lost its lease after many years, and the woman who managed the business could not sell the horses, equipment, or even the client list to the new operators moving in.

The manager decided to have a liquidation auction. She advertised and sent a sale catalog to every student, boarder, exhibitor, and guest who had visited the farm over the course of many years.

The horses were meticulously groomed, people turned out in droves, and the bidding was incredibly high. Everything sold, right down to the last pitchfork, for more than she expected. In many instances, current and former students bought the horses on which they had learned to ride.

Horse Auctions and Sales

Selling your horses through auctions or horse sales can save you time in setting up appointments and showing horses to customers. You'll make even more money if you stage the auction or sale yourself. If you are completely unfamiliar with horse auctions and sales, attend several before holding your own.

SELLING THROUGH A PROFESSIONAL AUCTION

To give you a better idea of how an auction works, I'll use information from a professional auction company as an example. This company advertises nationally and locally, and it publishes a brochure listing each horse it handles, which is sent to over 4,000 prospective buyers on a mailing list. It produces and mails to interested buyers a catalog that gives detailed information on each horse consigned in a sale.

Often, the seller gets these services for less than the cost of a few classified ads and pays less commission than an agent would charge. At the auction, the company advises that you put up displays and decorate your stall to draw attention to your horse. To get a good price, your horse should be healthy, fit, carrying good weight, and be well groomed.

You can set a minimum price on your horse so you aren't forced to take a low bid. If you sell the horse in the ring above your minimum price, you will receive a check from the auction company shortly thereafter.

Before going ahead, check out various auction companies with other area horse owners to make sure the one you select is reputable. They can also educate you about the various buyers that frequent auctions, and tell you which ones run operations where horses are well cared for and which do not. With this information, and by using your right to refuse a low price, you can minimize the risk that your horse will end up in bad hands or be resold by the pound.

HOLDING AN AUCTION AT YOUR FARM

By holding an auction or sale yourself, you can avoid sales commissions and entry frees. Your profits will include commissions and entry fees on horses you sell for others. Holding an auction or sale on your farm is also a great way to bring in new business. Those who come might end up as boarders and students.

Planning an Auction

To hold an auction at your farm, research local, state, and federal licensing laws or hire a professional auction company. Most states have stringent licensing laws for auctioneers and auction houses. If you hire a professional company, get recommendations from others in the horse business, and find a licensed and bonded company that has been in business for some time. A well-run company will have someone who consults carefully with you over the planning and operation of the sale.

Online Savings

With the high cost of postage, it is better to e-mail whenever possible and mail just the catalog. If you find that many people receive the catalog but don't actually intend to buy horses, you may need to start charging for the catalog to cover your printing and mailing costs or send the entire catalog online.

Promoting the Auction

Think about the audience you want to reach, and advertise in periodicals that reach that audience. And don't forget to advertise on the Internet.

Coordinate this advertising with a sequential mailing. The mailing announces the sale and enlists and informs consigners and buyers. It consists of a postcard, consignment forms, consignor's letter and information sheets, brochure, and a full catalog.

Sequence of Mailings

1. Send a postcard to announce the date of sale, and so on.
2. Mail consignors the forms that were requested. Also mail these forms to a regular list of consignors and anyone else who may be interested. You will need to have an attorney familiar with the horse industry provide you with a consignment form that protects you from liability. If you hire a professional auction company, it might provide this type of form. Be aware that liability laws differ from state to state.
3. Next, consignor's letters are sent to those who consign. See the consignor's information in appendix I on page 204.
4. Send a brochure to your entire mailing list first class, to help you update your mailing list (if people have moved and the brochure is returned, you can remove their names). Respond to any requests for more information generated by the brochure.
5. Finally, the last part of the five-piece mailing — the full catalog — is mailed. It is sent to sellers, those who requested a full catalog, and a short list of "regulars." Review your budget and see if postal mailings are feasible. You may need to e-mail all of the pieces mentioned above.

Horse Sale Planning Calendar

Check with your local and state authorities to see what licenses or special permits may be required before planning the auction. Your auction company should be up to speed with everything.

SIX TO TWELVE MONTHS BEFORE THE SALE:

- Decide on the type of sale and your target audience.
- Book the auction company and ask for any suggestions on planning the sale. Schedule a rain date.
- Print your postcards, consignor's letters, and information sheets.
- Begin the five-piece mailing, sending as much as possible by e-mail.

THREE TO SIX MONTHS IN ADVANCE:

- Begin compiling catalog.
- Order the consignor's numbers.
- Secure the office staff, announcer, ring people, barn staff, sale veterinarian, runners, and gate person.
- Organize a concession stand and arrange for personnel.
- Obtain public address system or megaphones.

ONE MONTH IN ADVANCE:

- Mail catalog.
- Rent portable toilets, if necessary, and buy sufficient toilet paper.
- Provide adequate trash receptacles and arrange for emptying.
- Paint equipment (such as jumps) as needed.
- Ask local rescue squad emergency personnel to be on hand for the sale, if necessary. If you think there could be traffic congestion, notify the local police for assistance. A donation to the EMT and police department is always a nice gesture.

TWO WEEKS IN ADVANCE:

- Call to confirm the auctioneers, announcer, ring people, concessionaires, office and barn staffs, sale veterinarian, gate person, and runners. Give them directions and arrival times.

THE DAY BEFORE THE SALE:

- Disk and drag rings.
- Get change for the cash boxes, concessions, and tack shop.
- Mow grass.
- Set up jumps in practice ring.
- Put up signs and directional arrows.
- Clearly mark parking area, water faucets, sale office, and so forth.

SALE DAY:

- Check for negative Coggins tests.
- Make sure the jump crew knows when to change fences and to what height.
- Give auctioneers, ring people, and announcer food and drink throughout the day.
- Keep the sale moving along quickly.
- Pay all the hired personnel.
- Make sure all complaints are handled properly and all financial matters, including vet certificates and registration papers, are filed.
- Pray for good weather and a good turnout!

THE DAY AFTER THE SALE:

- Make sure all trash is collected.
- Return all rented equipment.
- Put all the money you made in a high-earning cash investment!
- Figure out when the checks will clear and prepare to handle registration transfers and other paperwork in the specified time period.
- Make a list of areas that need improvement for the next sale and follow through in making changes.

The information above should help you hold your own horse sale. Be sure the grounds are in excellent shape and really showcase your operation. If you have a tack shop, stock up on products that may be needed at a sale — shampoo, braiding equipment, fly spray. Enticing sales may bring an additional profit.

Have plenty of farm brochures with inserts stating services readily available. Camp brochures and horse-show schedules also should be plentiful. Make sure the announcer promotes upcoming events at your farm.

Other Elements in a Catalog

Catalogs often list personnel associated with the sale, including auctioneers, announcer, ring people, and sale veterinarian. In addition, the catalog should provide an index of consignors and an alphabetical index of horses to be sold at auction. The conditions of the sale can be printed on the inside back cover.

Your Catalog

Tailor your catalog to fit your specific situation. The cover of the catalog should include sale name, date, location, features, and information contacts. The inside cover should have welcoming statements, schedule, and sale personnel, as well as important notices such as:

- Please read and familiarize yourself with conditions of the sale. (You should obtain this from the auction company or your attorney.)
- There is no implied warranty made by the auctioneer as to the merchantability or fitness for particular purpose of any animal offered for sale in this auction. All responsibility lies between the consignor and the buyer.
- Prospective bidders are cautioned that warranties on horses purchased are only as stated in the conditions of sale.
- Veterinary assistance is available at bidder's expense on request to auctioneer. Examine horses before bidding.
- Buyer has the right to have a veterinary examination within 12 hours of the start of the session in which the horse sells and before the horse leaves the sale grounds.
- Registration papers will be mailed to the American Quarter Horse Association (AQHA) for transfer for Quarter horses and to the buyer for other breeds not sooner than 30 days after the sale for horses is paid for by check.
- All sales made on the sale grounds must be through the office.
- A paid receipt or release is required to remove any horse from the sale grounds.
- Visa and MasterCard (or whatever credit card you prefer) are accepted with a 5-percent buyer's premium.
- In states that charge sales tax, all sales are subject to being taxed unless buyer has a valid dealer's registration and signs a proper state tax form, or buyer signs state tax form that horse is purchased for breeding purposes only.

BREEDING HORSES

Establishing an active breeding program on your farm has good money-making potential, but be forewarned: It is far more complicated than simply getting two animals together for mating purposes and, without good planning, you could lose a lot of money.

Many horse owners, in an effort to extend the usefulness of their mares, go into the breeding business. They figure they can sell the offspring profitably; however, unless you are ready to invest substantial capital and unless there is a strong market for yearlings, this is a difficult prospect. Before you jump into the breeding business, therefore, put pencil to paper and figure out the costs.

Currently there are many unwanted horses being abandoned in this country, so be sure that there is a market for the offspring before you breed. Racing Thoroughbreds and Standardbreds are best suited for this type of business.

Breeding Costs and Challenges

Be aware of problems that can occur with breeding your horse. These might include:

- Mares on fescue grass are at high risk for delivery problems and difficulties producing enough milk.
- Foals who don't get the mares' colostrum (first milk) need plasma and much veterinary care, which can cost $1,000 in the first few days of their lives.
- If they become toxic, the bill can be in the thousands and the foal may still die.
- Contracted tendons and dummy foals, who didn't get enough oxygen, can also be costly.
- There is always the potential of losing both the mare and foal at the time of foaling.

Be sure to count the potential costs and challenges before breeding your mare.

There are two ways to breed. Either you breed your mare to a stallion owned by another party or have your stallion bred to someone else's mares. The latter tends to be the more profitable of the two types of breeding.

Breeding Your Mare

Suppose you own a $3,000 mare and you want to breed her.

- You breed her to a stallion whose stud fee is $900.
- The costs of caring for the mare while she is being bred total $300 (if she catches the first time you send her).
- It costs roughly $1,000 to maintain the mare for the 11-month gestation period.
- Delivery goes smoothly and you don't have to call in the veterinarian. When the foal hits the ground, you already have $2,200 invested.
- It will be 2 years before you can begin to train the horse to saddle, at a conservative cost of $2,500.
- Upkeep on the horse while you break it yourself, or send it away for training, costs another $700.

  Your total investment = $5,400

This is the estimated amount that must be invested in your 2-year-old horse. It could be higher or lower according to your particular situation, but the estimate here is conservative. The total selling price you'll need just to break even is more than the cost of the dam. The colt still must be shown, promoted, and advertised before it can be sold, and that costs money, too.

Breeding this mare and trying to sell her colt for a profit just don't make good financial sense. In general, the vast majority of owners will lose money in this situation. If you really want to breed one of your mares, consider the investment and potential profits or losses first. Don't make an emotional decision. Although your favorite mare has served you well, her most profitable future may not be as a broodmare in your barn. If you really want to keep her, you may be able to lease her out to someone else for breeding purposes. If she produces some real stars, take her back, breed her, and sell her offspring as yearlings.

Another option is to help offset the costs of a foal by using it as a teaching tool. This is covered in more detail under Integrated Systems on page 23. For example, you can hold a hands-on clinic, teaching students how to halter-break a foal, or a 6-month course on how to break a colt to saddle.

A Good Stallion: A Great Investment

If you have the right stallion and promote him properly, it should not take long to recover your investment in him.

Breeding Your Stallion

This type of breeding operation requires less capital and fewer (if any) mares. It can generate a positive cash flow in far less time. The primary source of income here is from fees paid by mare owners to have their mares bred to your stallion — the stud fee. Mares are brought to your farm, and their owners pay you for stud fees and mare care fees.

The principal goal of a completely commercial breeding operation is to breed as many mares as your facility and stallion can handle. Generally speaking, the commercial life of a stallion in this type of operation is 3 to 4 years in any one region. Although a stallion may still be profitable after that time, the demand for his services may begin to decline. The length of time during which a stallion is commercially viable will vary, depending on breed or horse type and the period of popularity.

Many breeders will combine both types of breeding. They will buy a stallion to breed to mares from other barns as well as their own. With most show-horse breeds, the most profitable operations breed largely to outside mares. This is especially true for small breeding operations; however, having a few good mares with foals in your barn is a good way to promote your stallion.

KNOW YOUR MARKET

Understanding the market means knowing first and foremost whether there is a demand for the type of stallion you want to buy and breed. What is the current population of this breed in the area? (National and state breed organizations, local horse councils, or the cooperative extension service can provide you with information.)

Research the competition by attending area breed events such as shows and races. What breeds are popular? What

Know Your Market

Before investing in the stallion-breeding business, have a thorough grasp of the market, stud-fee determination, and promotion of the stallion.

You can't expect to take a share of the market if you price your horse out of his league.

are their stud fees? How many mares were bred in the previous season? Much of this information is available in newsletters or simply from talking to people. Try to learn as much as you can from mare and stallion owners.

After you have completed your research, plan your marketing strategy. Review the information you have to determine whether there are gaps in the area's stallion market; these gaps might be for specific types of horses, horses with certain bloodlines, or stud fees for types of horses within a particular range. For example, there may be several stallions of a certain type in one region, but all are standing for high stud fees. You may be able to fill a niche in that market by standing a stallion of similar quality for a lower fee.

If there are no gaps, look for areas in the market in need of a good horse. A good example of this situation is in the cutting-horse industry. There are now many daughters and granddaughters of the great horse Doc Bar. Many stallions in the cutting-horse industry are sons and grandsons of Doc

Breeding horses is dangerous business! Make sure your experienced handlers, not the clients, are holding the horses.

Bar. The owners of the Doc Bar mares are looking for good stallions with different bloodlines to which they can breed these mares. Some breeders who saw this trend developing introduced into the market the right kinds of stallions and are now reaping the benefits of their foresight.

Consider the demand for young horses of the type you want to breed. What would be the market value of your stallion's "get" (offspring)? At what age will they bring their best price? For answers, read about or attend public auctions.

Purebred consignment sales can provide substantial information about the value of different types and ages of horses. If you're interested in a special type of horse (dressage, five-gaited, for example), find out its average sale price. Some auction companies will provide you with sale price averages and ranges for the various horse types they handle.

STUD-FEE DETERMINATION

The number of mares booked to your stallion will depend largely on the stud fee. The lower your fee, the more mares you'll breed. Assume that you have just bought a stallion, Silver Lightning, a popular sire in the West, and that you will bring him to the East Coast for the next breeding season. You may be tempted to think, "Silver Lightning bred 50 mares and his stud fee last year was $1,500; there should be no reason that he can't do that in the East."

More often than not, however, that line of reasoning results in a shortage of outside mares coming into your barn. Although Silver Lightning may be an exceptional horse that is widely known throughout the West, most people elsewhere will not know about him at all. If you charge a special introductory fee of $850 to $1,000, you stand a better chance of breeding him to a larger number of outside mares.

The same logic applies to the young stallion that has not had the chance to prove himself as a sire. In fact, you may have to keep the stud fee low until his offspring have the opportunity to prove themselves. The only exceptions may be stallions that have earned a reputation as outstanding performers in the show ring or on the race track, and owners of stallions who would prefer to breed a smaller number of mares the first year or two.

Image Sells Value

"An ounce of image is worth a pound of performance." That old saying is as true in the horse business as it is anywhere else.

Special Discounts

Few stallion owners charge the full stud fee for all mares. Most will give certain discounts for mares who are proven performers or producers of foals that have been successful in the show ring or on the racetrack; owners who book several mares to your stallion; and local mare owners or members of local clubs or organizations.

A special situation exists for the stallion owner who is looking for a particular type of mare to breed. If you are breeding hunters, jumpers, cutting, dressage, or reining horses, consider giving discounts to the members of the national and regional organizations that promote the particular type of horse you want.

You may consider increasing the stud fee if you reach or surpass your goal for the number of mares booked to your stallion the first year. This would certainly be the case if, during the first season, you had more mares than your program could easily handle. While your first impulse may be to increase the stud fee considerably, don't do it. Increase the fee gradually.

Let's go back to the example of Silver Lightning. Assuming that you reach your goal for the number of outside mares bred, you may increase the stud fee by $100 to $200 without losing many bookings. You can continue this annual increase until the first year that the stallion does not reach your breeding goal for outside mares.

If you still have people breaking down your door after increasing the stud fee gradually, you can raise the price more rapidly. On the other hand, you should maintain the stud fee at its current level after any year you fail to meet your goal for the number of mares booked to your stallion.

Consider the following when setting stud fees. The importance of each will vary with the individual situation.

Competition

What stud fees are stallions of similar quality earning in your region? This is a time to put aside your ego and personal preferences and take an objective look at your stallion.

The Mare Population

How many potential customers do you have? Many stallions and few mares could create a "price war," or it could force many stallions out of the market. On the other hand, a large population of mares that are potential crosses for your stallion may enable you to pick and choose.

When considering the mare population, try to predict how far people will be willing to haul their horses to breed to your stallion. A larger geographical region will obviously provide you with a larger number of potential customers. Do not assume, however, that your stallion will attract mares from great distances.

Keeping mares off fescue grass will avoid many foaling and lactating problems.

Mare Quality Means Foal Quality

If your stallion is valuable enough to attract quality mares, you may prefer to breed a smaller number of good mares per year. You can reduce the number of mares by advertising a higher stud fee or a stud fee arranged by private treaty. Generally, the mares eliminated from your stallion's book will be mares of lower quality. A reduction in the number of mares bred per year may reduce your annual income, but foals by your stallion will be worth more money if they are coming from better quality mares.

A blood test will check that the foal received adequate colostrum to prevent infection.

Your Stallion's Offspring

It is important to look at the show or race records of horses produced by your stallion and to know the selling prices of these horses. If you price the stud fee at $2,500, but the foals are only bringing $1,500, you're going to lose much of your business. If the stud fee is $500 and the foals are selling for an average of $1,500, you'll be in a significantly stronger position as you develop the marketing strategy for your breeding program.

Pros and Cons of Financing

Offering financing on stud fees will allow for income from your breeding operation to be spread more evenly throughout the year; however, if your breeding operation produces only a marginal profit or no profit at all, financing a majority of the stud fees may prove to be a disadvantage. You may not have sufficient cash flow to pay the extra bills incurred during the breeding season. Under these circumstances, it's a good idea to require payment of the mare-care bill when the horse leaves your farm.

With a financing plan, more customers may choose to breed their mares to your higher-priced stallion, hoping for a top-quality foal.

FINANCING

Some owners may want to breed their mares to your stallion but can't afford to pay stud fees all at once. Many of these potential customers will book their mares to your stallion if you allow them to pay the stud fee in installments. Financing the stud fee has become an increasingly popular practice over the last few years and will be used more frequently in the future. If you think offering financing will bring in more mares, try it.

There are a number of financing plans. You can divide the fee into three payments, with the first one due when the mare is booked, the second due when the mare leaves your farm, and the final payment due when the foal is born. Alternatively, you might use a more conventional financing schedule that includes a down payment and monthly, bimonthly, or quarterly payments over a certain period of time. You must also decide whether to add interest charges.

If you feel that a standard plan will not be sufficient for all of your customers who want to finance the fee, consider arranging financing on an individual basis or offering your customers a choice of two or three plans.

The value of financing the stud fee is partially dependent on the stud fee itself. Many people will use financing to breed their mares to higher-priced stallions that they feel will give them better foals. This line of reasoning may even hold true for stallions with stud fees of $500 or less.

If you do offer terms, finance the stud fee only. Be sure to have a financial plan and understand your cash flow position before making these decisions.

PROMOTING YOUR STALLION

You may own an outstanding stallion, but if you can't project that to your potential customers, your stallion won't have the opportunity to be proven as a sire. Remember, design all promotion to provide the maximum exposure for your stallion at the lowest possible cost.

An effective marketing strategy is the cornerstone of many successful breeding operations. It is not something that is done in a haphazard manner if you want to maximize cost effectiveness. Instead, organize your approach.

Analyze Your Stallion's Assets

Examine your stallion's assets before planning your promotional campaign. This analysis should be based on pedigree, performance, conformation, disposition, and producing ability. An attractive stallion with a strong pedigree and impressive performance and siring records will be the easiest horse to market; however, this situation rarely occurs, which means that some extra work will have to go into your promotional campaign.

Promote Your Breeding Operation

In addition to implementing the ideas for advertising and promotions outlined in chapter 2, there are three options to consider for the breeding operation: stallion service auctions, futurities, and promotional syndicates.

Stallion-service auctions. Your area breed organization may sponsor a stallion-service auction each year as a fundraiser. Stallion owners each donate a service by their stallions to the highest bidder to raise money for the organization. Each owner must breed a mare free, but all get promotional mileage in the process. The donation does not include mare-care costs; the mare's owner is still liable to the stallion owner for these expenses. The stallion owner makes a profit from care of the mare.

These auctions can be set up in different ways. Some groups hold them as result auctions, where you bring your stallion. This arrangement benefits the unknown owner or unknown stallion. More mare owners will have a chance to see him at the auction than if he stayed at the farm. If the stallion-service auction is operated in this manner, your stallion will get great exposure.

Other methods of conducting a stallion-service auction include a mail bid system and an auction connected with a social event.

Auctions can be effective for promoting your stallion. If you can't bring him there, at least attend and spread the word:

- Mount several pictures of your stallion and his offspring on bulletin boards
- Set up a table displaying promotional materials
- Show slides or a video presentation of your stallion

Tips for Listing Stallion Assets

- Study the pedigree. Get as much information as you can concerning the performance records of your horse's ancestors for at least three generations. If the only well-known horse is a great-grandparent, still include him in the list of assets for your stallion. While the record of an ancestor three or four generations back is usually of little genetic value, it does have marketing value.
- Look at your horse's lifetime performance record. If he was most successful as a young horse (weanling or yearling), make sure you add that to the list. State and national awards look good in advertising.
- Emphasize the strongest points of your stallion's conformation. List any superior conformation traits he passes to his offspring and his offspring's performance records.
- Don't forget disposition. This characteristic is especially important for many mare owners.
- Set long- and short-term goals for your stallion (see chapter 1).

Shop Local for Insurance

Save money on liability insurance. Your local insurance agent may be able to provide the same amount of coverage for considerably less than a national company can. Shop around. See chapter 3 for more on financial management of your business.

Most stallion-service auctions provide a catalog of their stallions. Have a good picture of your horse published and, using a footnote, acquaint the public with his strengths by listing pedigree, performance, and sire record.

If your local breed association doesn't have a stallion-service auction, generate some interest and start one.

Futurities. A futurity is a race or a show in which the horses are entered before they are born. The sire and/or dam is nominated in advance so that the foal can enter the futurity. Payments are then made periodically by the person who nominated the foal until the event takes place. Often, the owner of the mare will nominate the foal, pay into the futurity, and show the foal with the hope of winning money.

Many futurities are worth large purses. For example, the All-American Futurity is one of the world's richest horse races, and the winner takes home over $1 million. There are also halter, cutting, reining, and pleasure futurities for many stock horse breeds. There are even futurities for Welsh ponies. The races and shows may operate at the local, state, regional, or national level.

How does a futurity help promote your stallion? The answer is simple: People would rather win money than ribbons. By breeding their mares to your stallion, they have a chance to win money.

Be an enthusiastic supporter and promoter of futurities. As you work to stimulate interest in them, interest in your stallion will also increase, especially if he sires futurity winners. Make sure any advertising or promotional literature about your stallion includes the names of the futurities in which your stallion's offspring are eligible.

Promotional syndicates. An event that is starting to gain prominence, especially in the Quarter Horse industry, is the promotional syndicate. Several owners own one stallion and share costs and profits. Special cash awards are offered to winners of certain events exclusively for the offspring of the stallions in the syndicate. More information about syndicates can be obtained by talking to breeders and veterinarians who service breeding.

YOUR OWN CARRIAGE BUSINESS

Opening your own carriage business may be a great way to diversify your equestrian operation and bring in extra revenue. As more and more people move from rural areas into cities, there is an increasing desire to maintain that country connection, and consequently carriage businesses are growing in popularity.

Also, as the population of the United States continues to diversify, there are increasing opportunities to bridge cultures through the use of horses. People from around the world still desire to celebrate their age-old cultural customs using horses at weddings and various other ceremonies. This is an emerging trend with a broadening future.

Selling the Romance

Carla and John Hawkinson, whose expertise I've drawn on in this chapter, own and manage a carriage business based out of their Echo Brooke Farm in the Great Smoky Mountains of Tennessee. These lines appear on their brochures:

"Clip clop down a shady lane. Slow your pace of life. Enjoy the beauty of the Great Smoky Mountains in the cozy comfort of a horse-drawn carriage. . . ."

Selecting Horses and Equipment

It is beyond the scope of this book to go deeply into buying and training carriage horses, and fortunately, there are many good books available on the topic. Here I'll just address some business aspects of this type of enterprise.

Selection of good, trustworthy horses is imperative. Buy trained driving horses with farm and road experience. These horses know about hard work and are willing to stand — a driving horse's best speed! This is no business for green or inexperienced horses. If a horse proves untrustworthy in any way, move him on. Business is business and the safety of the client is your first concern.

VIRTUES OF DRAFT BREEDS

Not only do draft horses tend to be calm and even-tempered, but they will also save you money on feed bills. Many carriage businesses use draft horses that require only hay — no grain, no supplements — and their animals look great.

WEDDING HORSES

If you intend to offer carriage rides for weddings, be forewarned. Brides ask for white or gray horses — and they are beautiful — but day in and day out, they are double the work to keep clean. People can enjoy black horses just as much!

Don't make the mistake of promising a bride a particular horse or particular horse color. If you do, that's the very horse that will be missing a shoe on wedding day. Instead, promise an upscale service, professional in every way, with immaculately turned out horses and vehicles and professional staff. Sell the service, and then follow through. No one will be disappointed.

PONY CARTS

If you don't want to do the "big horse thing," it is possible to make money at birthday parties by giving pony cart rides.

And these are not just for children, either. I was once part of an extravagant celebration where the birthday person, who worked for a travel agency, was given different modes of transportation throughout the day culminating in a surprise birthday party on a train. She traveled on a motorcycle, sailboat, helicopter, and in my little pony cart before boarding the train.

Be creative; think of as many ways to market your product as possible. Get the word out and give those rides!

QUALITY EQUIPMENT

Whenever possible, purchase new equipment and maintain it. Buy the best you can afford. As well as presenting a professional, high-quality appearance, it will give you confidence. A vehicle breakdown is a nightmare.

What to Offer

Once you have your carriage business up and running, there are countless opportunities for your services. Below are some ideas others in the industry have proven to be successful.

ROMANCE IS IN THE AIR

The sky is the limit when you're dreaming up ideas for romantic occasions. Couples want something unforgettable and are willing to pay for it. For example, you can charge $300 for a one- to one-and-one-half-hour carriage ride that includes complimentary finger food and two splits of champagne. You may transport the bride, groom, or both to the wedding site, take them from there to the reception, and/or carry them to a romantic destination afterward.

Here are some other ideas:

- Gourmet country picnic with complimentary basket
- Candlelight dinner
- Moonlight ride
- Marriage proposal carriage ride — counsel clueless young grooms ahead of time on what makes it special for the bride (her favorite flowers, their special place, and so on)
- Anniversary rides
- Destination weddings

Photography

Taking good equine shots is a skill regular wedding photographers may be lacking. Providing quality photographs can bring in added revenue. Obtain written permission forms from your clients if you might want to use the images in your advertising.

Consider a Cultural Wedding

A popular new trend is to offer the special dress and type of horse or carriage used in various countries for an international wedding. In a Hindu wedding in India, for instance, the splendidly dressed groom makes a dramatic entrance on a white horse (or, often, an elephant). Indian-Americans may be interested in re-creating the wedding traditions of India in this country on their special day.

An Irish-American wedding, on the other hand, might involve a gypsy wagon or other horse-drawn conveyance carrying traditional musicians, serenading the happy couple.

Make a Classy Impression

If you offer a five-star carriage ride, you will receive five-star wages and tips for your services. Everything must be immaculate, every time. Bathe the horse before each ride, polish his hooves, make sure the tack is shining and the tux (or whatever professional attire is appropriate) freshly pressed. Your entire outfit must be spic and span if you want to retain the business of a top-notch establishment.

Prom Transportation

High-school students love to show up at the prom in unusual modes of transport. Your horse-drawn carriage might be just the ticket. Hang a poster at the high school, send a brochure to the parent association, or leave a business card at venues that host such events.

Have a photographer on hand on the big day, and send a photo to the newspaper the next day.

CITY AND HISTORIC TOURS

Offer city tours, historical tours, and special events. Do some sleuthing to see what is already available and come up with some service that isn't being offered. Research what historical event occurred or famous person was born in your area.

In London, for example, there are midnight "Jack the Ripper" tours ending at a pub that was one of his haunts. They also offer tours featuring writers, such as The Shakespeare Tour, giving an educational background as you view places like the Globe Theater.

It might be possible to trailer your horse and equipment to a specific historical location and book the entire day with different groups meeting you there so that, even if it isn't

If you live in a historic area, a carriage business can be a unique attraction for tourists.

close to your place, it will pay for itself. Maybe a local fox-hunting club, horse show, or race will let you give the non-horsey bunch a ride around the event. You can educate them on the finer points of horse events while they sip champagne and eat brie and paté from the safety of your carriage. You could even have available some event clothes such as helmets or cowboy hats, depending on the event, in which they can have their photos taken, for a profitable fee, of course.

Share Your Skills

In addition to offering transportation services for various events, you can use your skills, horses, and equipment to train horses and people in the dying art of driving.

SPECIAL EVENTS AND OCCASIONS

Your town may be celebrating the anniversary of its founding and want to remember its historic roots. Your carriage would be the perfect touch: research the era and develop an appropriate costume, accessories, and decorations.

How about renting out your carriage ride to advertise a particular business during the Fourth of July or other holiday parades in your town? Some companies would gladly pay big bucks not to have to do their own floats and still have the exposure for their company in the parade. Advertise that you can pull the wagon with the company's name on the side to celebrate its 25th or 100th anniversary.

Many towns and villages put on a special celebration in early December as an opportunity for visitors to get into the holiday spirit and browse the shops. With the streets closed to car traffic, this event might involve candlelit luminaries, seasonal refreshments, strolling carolers — and horse-drawn carriages transporting revelers.

Another option at the holidays is to deliver Christmas trees by horse-drawn carriage or sleigh to town squares or individual holiday parties.

For a more solemn occasion, a funeral procession offers a traditional farewell to a loved one. One of the most beloved horse vets in Virginia, Dr. Olive Britt, was taken to the cemetery, appropriately enough, in a horse-drawn carriage.

Partner Up with Quality

Partner with high-quality established bed and breakfasts, restaurants, hotels, and resorts. One of the best ways to ensure a great clientele is to associate with one of the finer

Setting the Price

Weddings generally have set prices for their rides. Check around online to see what other people are charging so you don't price yourself out of the market.

For transport carriage rides you can charge $500 for two to four people; eight-passenger rides go for $600.

hotels or resorts in your area and do their carriage rides exclusively.

Top-of-the-line establishments often join Relais & Chateaux, an association of world-class hotels and resorts with accompanying five-star restaurants. Search for them on the Internet to see where they operate around the world. Check to find one near you with whom you could partner your carriage business.

Find your favorite local or nearby establishment online, search for its most recent listing, and write the manager a letter offering your services, tailored to his or her every desire. Follow it up with a phone call and visit — or better yet, a carriage ride! You may be just what they have been looking for.

WORK WITH BOOKING AGENTS

Destination weddings, vacations, family reunions and packages to resorts can be a good source to ferret out markets. Look online at wedding and "vacations made easy" sites and see what you can negotiate with some of the booking agents.

Consider offering them a 20 percent discount so they can sell your carriage rides at the same advertised prices. Usually, these come with a voucher. Once the client has cashed it in, you fax the voucher back to the booking agency and it cuts you a check.

Promoting Your Carriage Business

Once your business is up and running, you'll need to promote it vigorously to make sure people hear about you. See chapter 2 for more on advertising and image building.

CREATE A PROFESSIONAL WEB SITE

An attractive, professional Web site will become a primary marketing tool. If you don't have the skills to do it yourself, hire a professional to create it for you, using your best photographs.

Carla Hawkinson says that her Echo Brooke Farm Web site brings her an enormous amount of business. "The key," she advises, "is to be linked to other people's sites. You get free advertising on the Web through companies with other things to sell, and if you put their link on your site, they will cross-link for you free."

Search engines will connect you to other links. Google will put you on free so, consequently, other people pay for your presence there.

DESIGN YOUR OWN CARDS AND BROCHURES

Design your own business cards and brochures online and have the online vendor print them. If you are artistic and want to do the entire piece yourself, you can buy software online so that you can design and print from your home. Some vendors have pointers for layout design and more. See chapter 2 for more information.

Business cards and brochures must be of especially high quality to appeal to a high-end market. (Use good paper stock, and be sure to proofread!) Of course, a carriage business can produce wonderful photos that will appeal to your audience at least as much as the words do.

Don't put prices on your brochure; have prospective customers refer to your Web site. This will enable you to change prices without having to reprint the entire brochure. It also leads them to new products you may be carrying that aren't in the brochure.

ADVERTISE IN YOUR LOCAL WEDDING GUIDE

Almost every town has a local wedding guide, often appearing as a newspaper supplement in fall or winter. Carla Hawkinson reports that Echo Brooke pays $1,000 a year for a single ad and receives more inquires from it than from any other source of advertising. "This one ad creates a presence for our carriage rides," she says, "so that whenever someone opens up the wedding guide, they see us. Then, when they are planning their weddings, they call us. Even though it is just for weddings, you can also promote family picnics, anniversaries, proposals, and family reunions to increase your business."

Bridal shows usually are not an effective place for advertising, in Carla's experience, because she doesn't want to waste the entire day just standing around with her carriage

Where to Place Your Brochures and Business Cards

Brainstorm about outlets to market your business, and then keep them restocked as needed. Consider, for example:

- Chamber of commerce office
- Tourist center
- Tack shops
- Feed stores
- Post office
- Library
- Wedding stores
- Tux-rental stores
- Dry cleaners

Befriend Your Competition

"Make friends with your competition," suggests Carla Hawkinson of Echo Brooke Farm. "They give us lots of referrals when they are too busy to do the rides themselves. We send them our overflow as well. Subcontract with them and give them a 75 percent booking fee."

and horses. For you, on the other hand, it might be helpful for networking at the start of your business, to get your name and face out there and make contacts. After that, just leave some of your cards at your friends' tables, and go make money giving carriage rides elsewhere.

If you decide to do a bridal show, often the organizer will waive the booth fee if you will give carriage rides out front in the parking lot — which is your best advertising anyway. Hand out lots of cards.

NETWORK WITH PROFESSIONALS

Network with wedding facilities and wedding planners, and give them a $100 booking fee for every customer they send your way. Soon they will begin to suggest the carriage rides in their packages. It is easy money for them and brings you a client you might not otherwise have.

OFFER PACKAGES AND COMBINE SERVICES

Work with a local restaurant or tea room to offer candlelight dinner rides and gourmet country picnic rides. Think of "add-ons" that will make you extra money — flowers, photography, setups for champagne — and be creative. Offer something that is uniquely you!

Carriage Business Resources

There are many resources available to you as you consider getting into the carriage business and to help you continue to make it successful. Use a search engine or look in Appendix L for Web sites and links for Rural Heritage, Carriage Operators of North America (CONA), and others.

TACK, EQUIPMENT, AND TACK SHOPS

Whether you're just getting started or you're adding to or replacing tack, buy quality equipment, new or used.

Tack and Equipment

Your tools are your tack and your equipment, and they are a vital part of every horse operation. Before running out to the first tack-shop tent sale of the season, however, sit down and determine your actual needs and your budget. Review the guidelines in this chapter and pick some items that fit into your management plan to save or make you money.

MONEY-SAVING TIPS

- Discount mail-order catalogs often have great deals on brand-name tack — but buy new only if you can't find it used.
- Ask your tack shop to give you a discount for the business you send to the store.
- Find and use consignment riding shops. They sell and buy used equipment and clothes, and usually have good prices.
- Organize an annual used tack sale/swap. Advertise at other barns in your area.
- Don't throw away old, broken, worthless tack. Even saddles with broken trees, scuffed boots, and cracked helmets can bring in money for display purposes. I sell display sets to department stores, Western wear stores, and Western-themed restaurants. You can do the same.

SADDLES

Buy saddles that suit your teaching needs. If you instruct riders in Hunter Seat Equitation, buy flat saddles, not deep forward-seat saddles with huge knee rolls. If you teach roping, you'll need Western roping saddles.

Quality leather will outlast you and your riding school and has excellent resale value. Cheap saddles and bridles are more likely to fall apart and can cause accidents.

HALTERS

Leather halters cost more than nylon halters, but they age better, especially if kept clean and oiled, and do not fray or fade. They also break more easily if a horse gets his back foot caught while scratching an ear or gets the halter hung up on something. Nylon halters with leather breakaway straps work well, too. This can prevent serious injury in the stall, the trailer, and the field. I worked with a horse that caught his halter on a large feed manger the night before a show. Somehow, he flipped over during the struggle to free himself. In the morning, we found him on his back with his head still attached to the feeder. The nylon halter withstood the violent struggles of a 1,100-pound horse. He pulled muscles in his neck and had to have stitches in his face. A leather halter would have broken, enabling the horse to free himself.

Horses generally should not be left in a stall with a halter on but, if they are, be sure the halter is leather or the nylon

Quality leather tack and equipment will outlast you and your riding school. It will also have excellent resale value.

type with a breakaway strap. The same goes for halters worn in the pasture: Use leather or a breakaway.

Try to find inexpensive, preferably used, leather halters. If you opt for the nylon breakaways with a leather head strap and the head strap breaks, replace it with an old leather belt you no longer use or an inexpensive one purchased at a thrift shop.

BLANKETS

Good-quality blankets that hold up are very expensive, so buy these used too, if possible, and keep them clean and in good repair so they'll last longer.

Before investing in blankets, consider whether you really need them. Most ponies and horses do not, unless they are clipped for show or are used heavily in winter. Remember: Once you begin blanketing a horse, you'll have to keep doing it all winter. If you blanket boarder horses, consider charging for the service because blanketing runs up your labor costs.

Before you pack up the blankets for the season, take them to your local Laundromat and wash them or take them to the car wash and power-spray them. Charge your boarders $25 to $35 for this service.

JUMPS

The most economical way to obtain good jumps is to make them yourself. There are blueprints available through your state cooperative extension service. Use a hard wood, such as oak, which lasts longer than other types of wood. Treat the feet of the jump with a wood preservative to prevent rot from constant exposure to the ground.

Jump rails can be quickly and inexpensively made. Purchase 12-foot-long (3.7 m) and 4 × 4-inch (10.2 × 10.2 cm) posts, and have the lumber mill saw off the edges. Mills usually charge only a few dollars each and can do it in little time. You might also be able to pick up free lumber if buildings in your area are being torn down.

If the thought of building your own jumps gives you chills, ask whether you can commission the local high-school shop class to build them for you. It will be much less expensive than having them built and shipped from a jump manufacturing company.

Make Your Own Clothes and Equipment

New horse equipment and riding clothes are expensive, particularly custom-made items.

Tack shops and horse magazines advertise books about and patterns for making your own riding clothes, horse blankets, and tack. If you are handy with a needle and thread, this can be a real moneysaver and moneymaker.

Monogramming is also popular with horse people. Everything from ratcatcher collars to horse blankets can be personalized. You may also wish to sell cross-stitched or embroidered name labels for chaps or dog collars.

Remember, if you sew just for yourself, you'll save; if you sew for others, you can add to your coffers.

Communal Property

Another way to save money on equipment is to have communal property. Get a few people to chip in and buy a horse vacuum or clippers. It's even possible to do this with high-ticket items such as tractors, mowers, or a hay baler. See whether others in the area are interested.

It may be worthwhile to have an attorney draw up some conditions to which everyone agrees. For example, decide who fixes it if it breaks, where it stays, how someone sells her share in the item, and so forth.

Trailers

When purchasing a horse trailer, try to buy a used one in good condition. Negotiate the price down as low as possible or do some trading. I once traded a very nice two-horse trailer for an older four-horse van plus a little cash. I had been able to buy the trailer at wholesale cost, so the trade value was actually much higher than the cash invested.

If possible, buy an aluminum trailer instead of a steel trailer. They are lighter, so your fuel costs are reduced, and they don't rust out.

EARNING BACK YOUR INVESTMENT

If you're doing a good business with your horses, don't buy a small trailer or you'll quickly outgrow it. Consider buying a four-horse trailer so you can take three other horses with you to shows and charge the owners a transportation fee. This won't cost you more time because you're going anyway and, with the extra income, you can quickly pay off your trailer.

If you spend $3,000 for a used four-horse stock trailer and average one show a month, hauling three horses at $45 per horse, in 2 years you will have made $3,240. Your trailer will be paid off *and* you will have hauled your own horse to the shows at almost no cost.

Make sure that the trailer pays for itself. Offer transportation services for horses, ponies, and equipment.

Good signage can inform your prospective clients of your new tack shop.

Opening a Tack Shop

It's easier than you may think. You don't have to open an enormous store if you don't want to, and you already have a built-in clientele, especially if you require riding helmets. You can develop a tack shop on your own premises — anywhere from an empty room in your house to an unused shed to a new structure.

ITEMS FOR SALE

Consider the capital involved in stocking your tack shop. Expensive saddles might earn you a higher profit, but you may not be able to sell them readily. If you can't sell expensive equipment in about 3 months, it may be wiser to stock your shop with less expensive items that move quickly.

What to Stock

Experiment somewhat to see which items sell well and which are harder to move. I remember buying a case of pine tar that sat in the tack room forever, as shampoos, fly sprays, and crops went flying off the shelves.

At a riding school, riding clothes do well, particularly for children who outgrow clothes on a yearly basis. Carry only a clothing-size line such as 6, 6½, 7, 7½, 8, 8½, 9, 9½, and 10 for boots; and a helmet-size line such as 6½, 6⅞, 7, 7¼, and 7½. This way, instead of having many helmets in inventory, you reorder only when one sells. You may find that you can get by on a more limited clothing-size line (6–7, for example), if your main customers are children.

To save money and space, carry one item in each standard size and reorder when necessary.

Make the Most of Your Tack Shop

- Keep overhead low; try to convert existing space into tack-shop space.
- Stock only those items that sell quickly, such as crops, a size line of boots, and a size line of helmets. Special-order large items such as saddles.
- Set up a sales display at the horse shows you attend.
- Sell used tack on consignment.
- Sell your barn T-shirts, sweatshirts, belts, and mugs. I have found that horse T-shirts sell well year-round. They make good nightshirts in winter.
- Sell paraphernalia from breed associations. Breed associations such as those for the Quarter Horse and Morgan horse have a variety of decals, posters, caps, and other gear available to promote their particular breed. Contact the U.S. Equestrian Federation (listed in appendix L, page 217), and see whether you can purchase merchandise wholesale.
- Buy horse-training videos. Have them available for rent or sale.
- Sell model toy horses.
- Sell horse books.

Before opening your tack shop, survey your clients and local farms to see what they would be likely to buy. Stay current with what disciplines and activities are popular in your region and provide what those riders will need. For example, stock safety vests in areas where eventing is popular.

Don't Forget the Fun Stuff

If many parents wait around for their children to finish lessons, consider stocking books and magazines about horses and other subjects they can read while waiting.

Gift items could be stocked, particularly around the holidays — books, videos, posters, magazines, monogrammed bracelets and other horse jewelry, model horses, T-shirts, pocketbooks, sweatshirts, and sweaters are good sellers.

Make a list of items that people ask for but that you don't have. Begin to stock these items so you won't lose the sale next time.

If someone wants to buy something that you're using just for display, such as a jump standard, sell it. It may be an item you want to stock in the future.

Where to Buy Stock

The products you want to sell come from two sources: directly from the manufacturer and from a wholesaler. You may need to establish an account with some places, which may be difficult if other tack shops nearby have accounts. Sources may require a large minimum order. But keep trying. The big trade shows, held all over the nation, display every product you could imagine. You can often get discounts for placing orders at the shows, and some "freebies," too. Check in horse magazines or call the manufacturers of some of the products you have bought and ask the name of the wholesaler.

Stock items that the shop frequently runs out of like fly sprays, ointments, braiding equipment, rain-helmet covers, umbrellas, hoof dressings, hoof picks, body brushes, crops, spurs, and gloves. Don't forget veterinary supplies such as bandages, antibacterial creams, wormers, shampoos and mane and tail conditioners, feeds and hay — if you have the storage facilities. Always have your tack shop open at shows, camps, and other events on the farm.

CONSIGNMENTS

In addition to new equipment, a moneymaker in your shop can be selling gently worn tack and clothes on consignment. With consignments you sell other people's tack or clothing and retain a fee for your services. Some tack shops are *only* consignment shops. This operation keeps your capital investment low. Here's a possible format:

1. Charge a consignment fee. Fees vary from about 20 to 50 percent. See what percentage your customers are willing to pay and adjust your fee accordingly.

2. Set a minimum number of days that you will consign the items, 2 months, for example; then the price gets lowered by 15 percent. If it hasn't sold in 4 months, return the item to the owner to avoid tying up valuable floor space.

3. Set a minimum value for the items you will consign, say $30. This eliminates your labor cost on low-dollar items.

4. Have the person come in and pick up the check or give credit; she will be more likely to spend the money made on a consigned item while in your shop, and you'll have a sale in addition to your commission.

You can also accept used saddles in partial payment for new equipment.

MONEY-SAVING TIP

If used items sell well, go to some auctions and try to get good deals on tack that you can resell for a profit. Just make sure the items are in good condition. I once bought a lovely bridle from an old horse trader. It was a brand new bridle but the studs were missing. I didn't notice this until I went to put a bit on, long after the sale was over.

Price your consignment items slightly below market value so they will move quickly.

How to Clean Up!

Another moneymaker is a cleaning and repair service for boots, chaps, tack, and blankets. This will bring more business into your shop. If you don't have the time or necessary equipment, contract the work out. Horse blankets can be cleaned quickly at a wand-type car wash, or you can buy or rent a power washer. Have a blanket wash day and charge everyone enough to cover the rental fee and a profit.

Be sure to use a soft nozzle so you don't blow a hole in the blanket!

TACK SHOP FINANCIAL/MONEY MANAGEMENT

Use the same principles of budgeting, cash flow, and planning discussed in previous chapters. Here are a few additional thoughts.

Separate your tack shop account from the rest of your farm so that you can see whether it is actually making money. Then, information for sales and income tax will be readily available.

Keep careful records of what goes to your riding-school stock from the tack shop. Bill the riding school and transfer money for payment of goods. When you can't find a crop when you need to school a horse, it's easy just to pop into the tack shop and "borrow" one. It should be accounted and paid for.

Keep a careful inventory of items and cash flow on your computer. Your accountant will need these receipts anyway, and they will be a good defense if the IRS comes to audit.

Pricing Stock

You may be wondering how to price items. Some products have a price suggested by the manufacturer. Books, for example, usually have the suggested retail price printed on the back cover. Other products normally have a 100-percent markup. You buy for $10 and sell for $20 to cover costs and make a profit.

Tack, however, generally has a lower markup. When you consider how long your inventory may sit on the shelf, even a 100-percent markup doesn't go as far as you might think when you take into account your mortgage, electricity, and insurance payments; staff salaries; and set-up costs.

Be competitive, but don't lose money unless it's part of a long-term plan to lure new customers. Check the prices at nearby tack shops. A "loss leader" is a product the store offers at its cost or at a loss to bring in new business. You may sell fly spray at cost and advertise your price just to get people into your store in the hopes they will buy something else.

Cash or Credit?

Cash is the best policy. Don't extend credit. Horse people, just as many others, tend to overuse their credit. Most customers will come up with cash or a check if they really want the item. Your creditors are not as kind; they expect you to pay up whether or not your customers do. This includes your own riding school. If you take credit cards, remember: These companies charge you about 5 percent of the sale price, so adjust your prices accordingly.

Layaway can be an attractive option to offer clients, but keep it short term.

Be Savvy and Save Money

Accurate record keeping is vital. Have a good computer system so you can instantly call up what and when you paid for an item. If someone comes in and offers you cash for an item at less than the price tag, check the computer. If the item has been sitting in the shop a long time tying up space and capital, it may be worth it to sell it for a little less profit so you can make room for some other products that are more in demand.

Make sure you tell your insurance carrier about your expanded business so that your coverage is complete for employees, tack, stock that you may transport to shows, items on commission, the computer, and your other needs.

ADVERTISING AND PROMOTING YOUR TACK SHOP

Many of the principles in chapter 2 also apply here. Have a grand-opening sale. Perhaps you can offer a special introductory 10 percent off all items ordered before the opening. Many wholesalers offer discounted pricing for items bought in bulk. The purchase of three bridles may reduce the price by 10 percent. If someone orders one and you order two more for the initial stocking of your tack shop, you make a profit and also get your store stock at a reduced rate. There is usually a shipping fee break as well. The more you order and have sent at one time, the more you'll save on shipping and handling charges. Watch your cash flow, however, to make sure you don't get in a pinch and overextend yourself for the month.

Don't forget the free advertising you get from publicity (see chapter 2). Send a press release announcing the opening of your tack shop.

Online Competition

Keep an eye out for competition on the Internet. If your clients usually buy products online and you can't match those low prices and make a profit, it might not be a good idea to open a tack shop. Alternatively, you could stock only impulse items and/or products that are quickly consumed, such as fly spray.

On the other hand, you can also do your own online sales and e-mail them to your mailing list. Or you can take orders and then order the products so you aren't tying up your money in inventory that just sits on the shelf.

MONEY-SAVING TIPS

Post a sign "exchanges only," and do not give cash refunds. This will prevent you from having to come up with money for refunds when you are short on cash.

Watch out for shoplifters. Be sure to have the tack shop staffed or locked at all times. Keep expensive, small items behind the counter. It's sad, but many things are actually stolen by disgruntled employees, not customers. "Opportunity creates a thief."

Have special sales and events — 10 percent off hunt nights, for example. Provide a spread of wine and cheese. On Dressage Day, have a dressage tea and 10 percent off dressage equipment.

TAKING IT ON THE ROAD

If you're going to shows anyway, take a line of items that are especially useful at competitive events. Think of what breaks, runs out, or is easily lost or forgotten: fly spray, wound ointment, rain covers, umbrellas, gloves, brushes, saddle pads, hairnets, reins, crops, coat show conditioner, hoof polish and applicators, leads, halters, buckets, and maybe one bridle. See what sells the best and, next time, take only those items to the shows. Shows provide an opportunity to try saddles on horses. Take one.

Have a nice display, maybe a canvas canopy or awning off your trailer. It doesn't have to be very large. Make sure the display is staffed at all times.

Take a few gift items for the poor non-horsey parents, such as, "I'm a Blue Ribbon Horse Show Mom," or "I hate horse shows" T-shirts as well as a rack of riding clothes. Remember, even if you don't make a big profit, you'll be at the show anyway, and you're publicizing your tack shop and farm.

If you don't want to add a tack shop to your enterprise but think you have the business, consider leasing out some space to an existing tack shop for a branch-type operation. Check with your insurance company to determine if, and to what extent, a tenant would be covered. If the presence of a second business doesn't change your premiums much and you find the right renter, you may be able to make money without having to do much more than sign a lease. Someone else will advertise, set up and run the place, and pay you for the space he is leasing, and possibly a percentage of the profits. That shop may even sell you tack at its wholesale cost.

PART III

Keeping Your Property Profitable

FARM PROPERTY AND MAINTENANCE

You may already own or lease land for the site of your home business and have all the space and facilities you need. If not, the first section of this chapter is for you. If you have already established your horse business, the latter part of this chapter will help you maintain your farm as cost-efficiently as possible.

Remember that even if you hire a real estate agent to help find your property, the agent may be paid by the seller. Have a local attorney familiar with all legalities affecting the horse business in your area brief you, check things out, and help you plan your business to abide by all laws and regulations.

Don't forget, you'll need a title search to be sure you have clear ownership.

Shopping for Property

To thrive, horses need adequate pasture to graze and space to move around. They will need shelter from bad weather. If you plan to stable them, they will need adequate indoor space. Buying land to build a farm or leasing an existing farm is no small investment, so you'll want to make sure you make a good selection.

More details are provided later, but keep the following important considerations in mind as you evaluate properties:

- Size and type of horse business you plan to have, including expansion plans
- Types of facilities you'll need, such as indoor and outdoor riding rings, a stadium, or cross-country courses
- Location, including public services, such as garbage and sewer, adequate water, and easy access to trails
- Proximity to neighbors
- Population in the area and whether it's large enough to provide clientele for a horse business
- If you're considering taking over the site of an existing horse business, was it profitable and, if not, why? Did it have a bad reputation? Can you realistically overcome the problems your predecessor had?

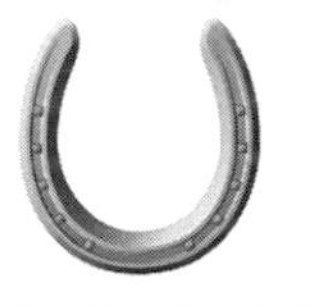

MONEY-SAVING TIP

You can make your business even more cost effective if you have adequate space and conditions for hay production.

SPACE REQUIREMENTS

Adequate pasture for horses to graze will keep your feed costs down and make your operations more cost efficient. In many areas, 2 acres per horse is ample, but if the soil and grasses are of poor quality, you'll need more. For example, on some of the rangeland in the Southwest, about 5 acres per horse is needed, but the land costs less than it does in other areas.

LAND CHARACTERISTICS

What aspects of a piece of property are less or more desirable for a horse farm? There are some specific characteristics to look for or avoid.

Trees and Shrubs

It would be preferable to have land with trees in the pastures to shade horses from hot sun and provide a wind break. Make sure, however, that the land does not have trees and

Advantages of Sandy Soil

Sandy soils are likely to make for easier going on horseback during wet spells, and they don't become compacted during dry spells, which can be hard on legs and hooves. Sandy soil is certainly better than heavier soil for riding rings.

Soil type can be important, but you may not have much of a choice. Generally, soil with a high percentage of sand will drain better than will soil laden with clay.

other vegetation that are poisonous to horses, such as wild cherry, yew, deadly nightshade, and red maple. Fruit trees, especially apple, could also pose a problem if horses eat too much of the fruit and develop colic or they choke on apples or other fruit. The shavings of black walnut trees, which one would be tempted to use for bedding, can cause horses to develop laminitis. Yellow star thistle is a rampant non-native, invasive weed in the west and is very dangerous. And if you have blister beetles in your area, be careful, especially with hay production.

Hills and Plains

Sometimes hilly land may be less expensive because it is not as suitable for development. It also provides good drainage if erosion is not a problem. If you are considering a hilly site, however, make sure there is enough flat land for buildings and rings.

Land in a floodplain can be a good value. Floodplains may extend for miles and provide extensive areas for trail riding without the threat of urban encroachment. A friend purchased pastureland in the 100-year floodplain in Virginia (the land had flooded in the last 100 years and, therefore, cannot be built on). She paid $7,000 an acre. Her sister

You may fall in love with a prospective property, but be sure to think through the pros and cons before purchasing it.

bought adjoining property that was not in the floodplain and paid $100,000 an acre!

Water and Fencing Subsidies

Considering that a horse drinks from 8 to 10 gallons of water daily, it would be advantageous to have a creek running through the property or a pond to help reduce labor and water costs, especially if you are paying by the gallon. Ponds, however, should be fenced off if you are in an area where winter temperatures reach the freezing point to avoid horses falling through ice.

Because of the increase in environmental concerns from animal waste polluting creeks and infiltrating drinking water, many states are now subsidizing the cost of fencing to keep animals out of the creeks and ponds. In southwest Virginia, where we live, you must already have a boundary fence on your property and cows in the creek for the government program to pay 75 percent of the cost of fencing the animals out of the creek. You must also continue to have livestock on the property for the next 5 years. In Tennessee, however, my sister-in-law received a check for $11,000 to help cross-fence her property; it really helped the overall plan of her farm as well. Check with your local extension agent or land grant university to find out about possible fencing subsidies.

BARNS

The subject of barns could take up an entire book, but there are some important points worth mentioning for anyone contemplating building or refurbishing a barn. It usually is less expensive to buy or lease property with an existing barn. Building costs today are high, especially if you can't do most of the work yourself. In some areas, the cost of a simple four- to six-stall barn can run $20,000 to $40,000.

If you do build a barn, try to make it compatible with the neighborhood architecture. Attractive paint colors and tasteful landscaping can make a less-expensive barn look better than it actually is, and it will please your neighbors. Architectural appropriateness will be more of an issue as farms become swallowed up in urban sprawl. My sister, for example, lives in a lovely Victorian neighborhood that has a

Floodplains: Reality Check

Bottomland in floodplain areas is usually very rich and can sustain more horses per acre than can higher ground, but there are pitfalls. If the land is wet most of the time, your horses could develop hoof problems such as cracking, thrush, and mud heels, not to mention pulled shoes. Mosquitoes, flies, and internal parasites could present problems.

The most obvious drawback is that you'll need to have an escape route if the area ever floods again. If the parcel is covered by the Wetlands Protection Act, an environmental law, you may be prohibited from building on it or clearing parts of it.

With all there is to consider, it is imperative that you check with local authorities to see what laws and regulations would affect the property and a horse business.

stable within the development. Normally, no one would paint a barn Victorian olive green, but that particular color makes this horse business fit in beautifully with its surroundings.

Also, visit large and small barns in your area. Notice what layouts work well, features (such as wash stalls) that are well used, and the size stall that seems to work best. If you are in an area with a cold winter climate, notice which barn designs retain heat. For warmer climates, consider barns that stay cool in summer.

OUTBUILDINGS AND OTHER FACILITIES

The list of other facilities and outbuildings could be a long one. Some of those you may seriously want to consider include a place to store hay if there isn't space in the barn; an office; and restrooms for clients, with a shower if possible. You may need a place to park tractors, trailers, and vans, as well as a parking area for clients, depending on the type of business you plan to operate. Other especially important considerations are outdoor shelter and fencing.

Well-laid-out facilities save labor costs by reducing the number of steps necessary to perform routine tasks.

Smart Barn-Building Tips

- Use low-maintenance, long-lasting materials, such as prepainted vinyl or aluminum siding instead of wood to save on repainting costs.
- Compare prices of products and contractors. Prices can vary dramatically from one supplier to another, whether you are shopping for lumber or an electrician.
- Plan for future expansion. A profitable operation will grow and require more space. Leave yourself plenty of growing room.
- Build it yourself or have students build it. The cooperative extension service has blueprints for small buildings available to you at no cost. In addition, many high schools have vocational courses in building trades. You may be able to have the students build the barn for the price of material only. Often, the school's shop teachers get supplies at a discount, so it pays to establish good relationships with local educators.
- Lay out plans to ensure a labor-saving facility. Centrally locate the feed room. Have openings in the stalls that enable the staff to feed and water from the aisles. My sister-in-law had a carpenter cut trap doors in the hayloft so that hay can be fed directly into the stalls. The trap doors are equipped with handles so that it isn't even necessary to bend over to open each door. This eliminates the need for hauling or tossing bales down and carrying them around.
- If you plan to have a lesson or stud barn, design stalls with doors that close in the aisles so that horses cannot reach out and bite when other horses are being led through. Have feed buckets installed so that horses in stalls next to each other will be on opposite sides of their stalls when eating; otherwise, it can cause tension and wall kicking. Design stalls so that the staff can feed through the stall wall without having to open the door, thereby risking injury walking a bucket of feed to the back.
- If you plan to include a washroom, invest in a brushed concrete floor to prevent slipping. To draw off water, include a drain, and design the floor to be elevated about 1 foot (0.3 m) above the outside ground level.

Outdoor Shelter

Horses that are turned out for long periods or that live permanently outdoors usually need a run-in shelter or trees. This protects them to some degree from sunburn and rain rot on their skin, and from hoof problems such as thrush, pulled shoes, and dryness and cracking. The main purpose of shelters, however, is to protect horses from freezing winds and driving rains.

Shelters should face south to avoid cold north winds. When I was growing up, my grandfather had a tool shed

An Efficient Rotation System

A horsewoman I know uses electric fencing to divide her pasture into small areas, rotating them every three days so that the crowns of the grass are never eaten below 3 inches. She had to feed only 30 bales of hay all last winter for three horses, compared to the normal rate of around 30 a month.

that faced north, and I converted it into a stable for my Shetland pony. In rainy weather, the pony could have stayed dry standing in the shed, but he preferred to stand in back of the shed to block the wind. In cold weather, I would often go out to knock icicles from his whiskers, lead him into the shed, and give him a warm bran mash, only to watch him promptly leave the shed and stand outside in the elements. My point is that horses would rather be wet than have cold wind blowing on them, so be sure to build shelters facing south.

The run-in shelter should be elevated enough so that the footing stays dry. It should be large enough to accommodate all horses that want to come in without resulting in a fracas. Usually, about 140 square feet (13.0 sq m) per horse is adequate for a run-in shed.

If you live where the weather is temperate most of the year, trees might provide adequate protection in cool and warm weather. You'll save on the costs of constructing a run-in shed, bedding for the shed, maintenance of the shed, and injuries that sometimes occur when several horses try to get into one shelter at once.

Proper fence maintenance saves on veterinary bills.

Fencing Options

There is a wide variety of fencing options available. The primary consideration, of course, is safety. Barbed wire is a poor choice because it can be a source of serious injuries to horses.

I favor wooden fences. They can be expensive and require regular maintenance, but they look very attractive running the length of a pasture. If you select wood fencing, be sure the rails are on the inside so that horses can't kick them out and to lessen the chance that foals will injure their legs on the posts. Oak is stronger than pine. Posts should be driven into the ground rather then using an auger to dig holes and tamping the dirt around them. This provides greater sturdiness and less labor time in construction.

Steel pipe fencing with steel posts is another good choice. Make sure the welds are smooth. Cover the entire fence with rust-proof paint. Instead of using a brush, apply the paint by rubbing it on with a thick rubber glove — it's easier.

Fencing Overview

Type	Maintenance	Pros/Cons
Electric	Low	Costs less than many other types of fencing. Requires power; horses could become impaled on low posts or entangled in wire.
Wooden	High	Attractive, but is high maintenance and can cost a lot. If not maintained, horses can become impaled on broken boards or injured by nails. They can also ingest wood if they chew on boards.
PVC	Very low	Requires virtually no maintenance and has few if any hazards. If horses bump into it, it gives. But it's very expensive.
Steel pipe	Moderate	Prices vary widely depending on the geographic location. Requires welding at posts. Must be painted periodically with rustproof paint and, if horses collide with it, it won't give.

Polyvinylchloride (PVC) is popular in some areas. It is sometimes installed with concrete posts and is virtually maintenance free, except for occasional power washing. The PVC rails "give" a little when bumped by horses, which reduces the likelihood of injuries.

Electric fencing can be effective in separating areas within a pasture, but I don't recommend it for widespread use around an entire field and especially wouldn't use it along a road. If horses are frightened and running hard, they'll go through the fence. If you have any electric fencing on your property, be sure to put up a warning sign for people.

Before investing in fencing, talk to other horse owners to find out which type seems to hold up best in the area's climate and which is the most economical. Then comparison-shop among fence vendors. When shopping for a four-board post and rail for 1,375 feet I received three estimates — $12,500, $10,000, and $8,000 — for the exact same fence. If you let your fingers do the walking, you may be able to get the materials cheaper, just pay for the labor, and come out ahead.

LEGAL CONSIDERATIONS

Before purchasing or leasing a site for an equestrian operation, check with the planning commission to see what the future holds for your area. What are the plans for sewer and water lines? Are there statistics indicating what the growth will be in the region? A rising population could help a riding-lesson stable by increasing the number of potential students, but it could hinder a public trail-riding stable if access to trails is lost in the course of developing housing.

Ask whether there are any livestock restrictions that could hinder your business operation. Has anyone else submitted plans to open a riding school nearby? Are there any major roads planned that would increase the value of the land and, therefore, raise your property taxes? This kind of change could bring in more business, or it could cut up your property and decrease its value or make the property worth more but raise your taxes.

In the long run, it may be more profitable to purchase land that costs more initially but is located in a more profitable area rather than buying a cheaper parcel that is so remote that there are not enough people around to support your business. The profit potential of the property's location must be fully investigated and projected before you make a purchase. Even the best book on farm-business management will do you little good if you have no clients.

After all these considerations, don't forget to learn about all the permits you'll need for an equestrian operation. Zoning regulations, building permits, environmental laws for waste disposal, wetlands regulations, and, if applicable, homeowners' association rules must be checked. Easements may exist. Where I live, there is a gas easement behind the house and, even though my husband and I own the property, there are restrictions about how close we can build and dig near that easement. Often, no one tells you these things; you must ferret them out yourself.

LEASING PROPERTY

If you don't have much money to spend on property, you aren't sure you want to be in the horse business forever, or you're not certain you can make a living with horses, leasing

Pros and Cons of Leasing to Buy

Leasing with an option to buy can be advantageous because:

- There are no closing costs or agency fees.
- Many banks will not make a loan of more than 50 percent if the property is raw land, or will charge a significant down payment or a higher interest rate. Sellers may be willing to finance the property to you regardless of the amount of raw land.
- Sellers may charge a lower interest rate and require less money down than would a bank. If the sellers are wary of such a transaction, demonstrate on paper how much more they can make with interest on the property, compared with what they would make if they sold through a real-estate agent and did not finance the property.

Lease-to-buy options can be disadvantageous when:

- The owner charges an interest rate that is higher than you can get at a bank.
- The owner allows you to borrow more than a bank would, the amount is more than you can afford, and you end up in default and the seller gets back the property.

may be a better idea than buying. Leasing with an option to buy may be the best choice of all.

Before signing a lease agreement, however, have your attorney review the documents to make sure they are to your advantage. I know of a case in which someone leased property and erected aluminum facilities with the intention of taking them down when the lease expired and moving them to their new property. This person found out too late about a clause in the lease stating that improvements made on the property would become part of the real estate and could not be removed when the lease was up. Make sure your lease stipulates who has the right to take any improvements with them when they leave.

"At Your Own Risk"

For your own protection, hang a disclaimer notice reminding people that you are not responsible for lost or stolen equipment.

Farm Management and Maintenance

It is essential to provide proper maintenance of your facilities. You'll reduce the number of injuries to horses, which helps keep veterinary bills in check. If your farm is nicely maintained, you also are more likely to keep clients and attract new ones.

BUILDINGS

Routinely check the barn and every stall in it for protruding nails, jagged metal, splintering boards, and anything else that might result in an injury to horses or to people. Check the locks on stalls and gates to make sure they are in good working order to prevent horse escapes.

Make sure the feed room is easily accessible for feeding as well as for deliveries, but install locks that will keep horses out.

Unfortunately, disappearing tack and equipment is a common complaint among boarders. Eliminate headaches by selling tack trunks or making available lockers in the tack room. Door and cabinet locks may deter would-be thieves.

LANDSCAPING

Landscaping around the farm can add significantly to its visual appeal. Be sure to take proper care of trees; fertilize and prune as necessary. Cover trees with heavy-gauge chicken wire or fence them off if the horses are chewing on

Quality landscaping prevents drainage into your barn and creates a professional, welcoming appearance.

them. (It doesn't take long for a horse to remove a strip of bark all the way around a tree, which will kill the tree.)

An attractive flower garden around the stables gives it a professional, welcoming appearance. Potted plants dress up jumps when you have horse shows.

With the high cost of groceries taking a greater portion of our budgets, it is wise to consider productive plants such as blueberry bushes and fruit and nut trees in your landscape design. Herb and vegetable gardens can also significantly reduce your grocery bill, and the surplus can be sold to your clients.

PASTURE MAINTENANCE

Establish and maintain good pasture. Remember, a well-kept pasture is an inexpensive feed source.

If you need help developing better pastures, contact your county cooperative extension service, which is affiliated with state-operated agricultural colleges. Your tax dollars pay for these services, so use them. Most extension agents have a wealth of agricultural knowledge and are ready to answer questions. All cooperative extension services have publications, videos, seminars, and youth programs; they'll also perform forage and soil testing.

Here are some basic pasture maintenance practices to follow.

Tidy up. Routinely check pastures (and paddocks) and remove any debris, dead branches, equipment, poisonous plants, loose wire, stones, and anything else that could prove hazardous.

Test your soil and improve it. Learn about your soil and fertilize as necessary. Your local extension agent can provide instructions, kits, and mailing boxes that enable you to test your soil and determine the quality of your pasture. This is not expensive; a test costs around $10 or, in some states, is free. Some nurseries and feed companies will test for you if you buy from them, but be sure they don't recommend more fertilizer than you really need.

Mow as needed. Mow pastures periodically to keep down weeds and seed heads.

Rotate. Practice pasture rotation to avoid overgrazing. Carefully monitor grass height and, when it starts getting short, move horses to another pasture.

Other animals can help. Grazing other species, such as cattle, sheep, or goats, helps break the parasite cycle. Some parasites are species-specific; even if a sheep ingests them, it won't be a good host for the parasites, which consequently will not reproduce. Different livestock also eat weeds and grasses that horses don't or shouldn't eat.

Keep horses on pasture. Provide pasture grazing throughout as much of the year as possible. Pasture boarding has very low overhead costs (if you don't have to irrigate or pay high taxes), and can be one of your more profitable services. It's also good for horses. Green grass and sunshine benefit horses mentally and physically, especially horses that are stabled often.

Plant wisely. Plant cool-season permanent species of grass (such as fescue, timothy, or bluegrass), summer perennials (such as Bermuda grass), and winter annuals (such as wheat, oats, or barley) to maximize the time horses get adequate nutrition from the pastures. Alfalfa and clover also are good additions. Check with your local cooperative extension service to determine the best planting schedule for your area and for help in choosing plants. Fescue, for example, has

To maximize the time horses get nutrition from the pastures, plant cool-season grasses (such as timothy) and summer grasses (such as Bermuda grass), along with winter annuals (such as wheat or barley).

Put Horse Power to Work

To contain labor and fuel costs and reduce wear on your tractor, train a horse to pull a drag and let students drive the horse over the pastures. You could have them drag rings and paddocks, too. Dragging the manure piles exposes the feces to the sun, which, in turn, reduces the number of parasites that ultimately could end up inside your horses.

Growing your own hay can save significantly on your feed bill but does require intensive labor several times a year.

been associated with spontaneous abortion in brood mares if ingested late in the pregnancy, as well as ending milk production.

Grow it yourself. Consider growing your own hay, if you have the land, and hiring a local farmer to cut and bale it for you. This may be economical, although if he waits and cuts his hay first and does yours late in the season, you may not end up with good-quality hay. Also, you will need a work crew to pick the bales up out of the field or a tractor with a spike to move the big round bales. Make a deal, dividing the bales 50–50 with the farmer or whatever percentage you can arrange, for the cost of mowing.

BEDDING

Bedding is a continual and often expensive necessity for a stable, so shop around for the best price. Feed stores are usually the most expensive bedding suppliers. It is more economical to go directly to the source, such as a neighboring farmer or a sawmill.

There are many types of bedding: straw, course sawdust, peanut hulls, wood shavings, and chips are good. Some companies are recycling newspaper for bedding. If available locally, it may be practical and inexpensive. Check to see whether the prices on different kinds of bedding change with the season and adjust your orders accordingly.

Make sure the wood products you use for bedding do not contain any toxic products such as Japanese yew or walnut.

FIRE SAFETY

Every horse owner fears a barn fire. Practice these safety tips to help prevent a catastrophe:

- Keep electrical systems clean and updated
- Hang certified fire extinguishers in readily accessible locations
- Plan and practice horse-evacuation fire drills
- Prominently display "no smoking" signs in the barn
- Remove combustible or hazardous materials from the barn
- Ask the fire department to inspect your facilities and make recommendations
- Install a pond; it can be used in case of fire, as well as for drinking and irrigation

Instituting a good fire-prevention program will reduce the risk of damage and accidents and may decrease your fire-insurance premiums. Be sure to tell your insurance agent about any preventive measures you have taken and ask how you can further reduce your fire-insurance premium.

SAVING ELECTRICITY

A great deal of electricity is wasted through carelessness. Being energy conscious will reduce the amount of electricity you use *and* cut down on your bills.

Electricity Conservation Tips

- Ask the electric company to send a representative to conduct an energy survey at your facility and make recommendations about how to conserve.
- Place "please turn off" signs wherever appropriate. Be vigilant about enforcing the policy.
- Put timers on the lights so they turn off automatically.
- Use low-watt light bulbs. Fluorescent lights are the most economical.
- Purchase light bulbs that have a lifetime guarantee. Many charities sell these bulbs to raise money. If they burn out, the charities will replace the bulbs free. Be sure, however, to keep your receipt and remember your contact.

More Bedding Moneysavers

- The less time that horses spend in their stalls, the less bedding they soil. This is another reason to keep horses outside as much as possible.
- Don't bed the stalls excessively. There will be less waste and less labor required to clean stalls.
- Make sure your barn help knows how to pick the stalls economically by removing droppings and wet spots, but not unsoiled bedding. Inspect their jobs periodically to make sure they are not wasting good bedding.
- Compost the soiled bedding and manure, then put it up for sale. Strip and lime stalls only when absolutely necessary.

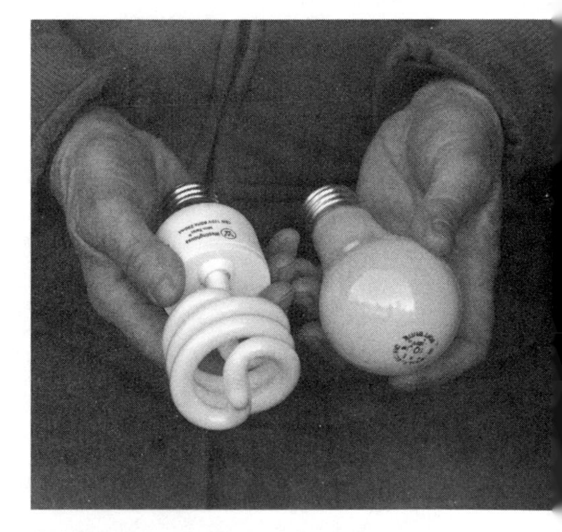

Compact fluorescent light bulbs (CFLs) use 75 percent less energy and last about 10 times longer than incandescent bulbs.

Conserving Water

Water is an increasing concern in certain parts of the country. As prices increase and reservoirs shrink, conservation becomes even more important.

- Water the rings when the water is least likely to evaporate — early morning or late afternoon is usually best.
- Repair all leaky faucets, hoses, and waterers immediately.
- Install or replace rubber washers as necessary.
- Limit the time allowed at the wash rack.
- Make sure the spray nozzle on the hose at the washstand works so that water isn't wasted when horses are bathed.

- The electric company can install mercury lights. These outdoor lights cover a large area and turn on at dusk and off at dawn. Mercury lights are also great antitheft devices. Be aware that the electric company might charge a monthly rate, so evaluate the cost effectiveness of this option carefully.
- If you do not need lights on overnight, consider installing lights that are activated by motion detectors.
- Remember to pass your electric costs on to your customers. If you rent your lighted rings out to the public, charge enough to cover your costs and make a profit.

CONSERVING FUEL

Fuel prices and taxes on fuel continue to climb, but you can save on consumption with careful planning. Practice good vehicle maintenance. Proper tuning, oil changes, tire inflation, and alignment all reduce oil and gasoline consumption. (See the Vehicle Maintenance Record in appendix H, page 203.) If you have an electric water heater, put a timer on it so that you heat water only when you need it. You could, for example, set the timer to turn off the heater overnight. Lower the temperature on the heater to 120°F if it is set any higher than that.

RECYCLING MANURE

Manure requires careful management for several reasons. Inadequate manure disposal results in unpleasant, lingering odors around the farm. It also attracts flies. Make sure your farm has a plan for handling manure; don't just throw it away, and certainly don't pay someone to haul it away for you. The production cost of manure is quite high, and manure has outstanding fertilizing potential. Make the most of it by composting and selling manure.

CONTROLLING FLIES

The two-winged menace known as the "fly" is annoying to both man and beast and must be controlled to keep a pleasant environment in your barn. Clean facilities and good manure management will result in fewer of these dirty pests. There are a number of systems available to help control fly populations.

REPELLENTS FOR STABLES

Some systems spray a fine mist into the stalls and aisles. With this system, a large barrel containing the insecticide is attached to a timer. Insecticide is released at certain intervals into tubing that sprays through nozzles into the barn. The insecticide is harmless to warm-blooded animals. Although this system is very effective, it can be expensive and may be financially viable only for larger operations. Other systems operate from battery-powered canisters that release a fine mist at timed intervals. These work well and are relatively inexpensive, but they require a periodic battery change.

Flypaper is still the most economical way to kill flies. Despite its unsightly appearance, it does do the job. You can now buy large (1- × 6-foot [0.3 × 1.8 m]) sheets. Attach them securely to walls and ceilings to eliminate contact with animals or people.

Liquid, environmentally friendly fly traps are also available. These are effective and safe but can be a bit nasty to smell and change.

FLY REPELLENTS FOR HORSES

In addition to controlling the overall fly population, the horses themselves must be protected from fly attacks, particularly horses at pasture. A horse's fretting causes stress and weight loss; these, in turn, cost you money.

There are a number of horse fly repellents on the market. The most economical products are usually concentrated and are generally found in feed stores and tack shops. Shop around for the best prices because fly sprays can be expensive. Be sure to dilute concentrated fly products as recommended by the manufacturer.

Consider feeding supplements with insecticide or providing insecticide blocks, although these options might also be expensive. Ask your veterinarian about the fly-control systems that work best in your area.

Provide your horses, and ask boarders to provide theirs, with fly masks, which keep flies off the eyes of horses. These work well in the pasture. You can make your own version of a face protector by attaching strips of cloth to the horse's halter.

Recycling Manure

- Sell the manure as a "self serve" — let customers shovel and remove it by the truckload or barrel.
- Deliver it to nurseries or private homes.
- Bag it and sell it at the local greenhouse.
- Spread it on your own hayfield or garden. Be careful not to spread it where horses are pastured; this can lead to parasite problems.

REDUCING VETERINARY BILLS

After managing an equestrian operation, having children, and writing the first edition of this book, I decided to go to veterinary school and become an equine vet. I am now able to look at horse health care both from the vantage point of having managed a horse business and now as a practicing horse veterinarian. So I would like to offer some insights to help you save on your horse's health care costs.

My clients say to me, "We love you guys, but we would rather not see you!" I don't take it personally because I know veterinary bills can take a huge chunk out of your profits. There are, however, some ways to significantly reduce your vet bills and still have healthy horses.

Prevention Is Thrifty

An ounce of prevention is worth a pound of vet bills. Spending wisely on good preventative vaccine and deworming programs designed specifically for your operation saves money in the long run, preventing expensive illnesses and poor health from parasitism. For example, the Eastern and Western Encephalitis and Tetanus vaccine is currently $9, whereas either one of those diseases with hospital stay could cost $5,000 — if the horse survives at all. One deworming can be $5, while colic from parasites could cost you from $200 to $10,000.

You can save even more money by learning to vaccinate your horses yourself. Let's look at the difference in cost reduction if you administer your own vaccines instead of paying the vet to vaccinate your herd. The chart on page 166 shows comparative costs of a combination Eastern, Western Encephalitis, Tetanus and West Nile vaccine and a separate Rabies vaccine. (These are the core vaccines recommended by the American Association of Equine Practitioners.)

I found these do-it-yourself prices online from Valley Vet. Anyone can order these vaccines; you don't have to be a vet. Just check your state laws.

Below I compare your costs against what a reasonably priced vet charges. You can see that by doing it yourself you save $75 for a single horse. If you have 10 horses, you can divide the cost of the farm call among them but you can also save more by buying larger quantities of the vaccine yourself. Vaccines for 10 horses will cost you $500 from the vet (including the farm call), whereas you can administer them yourself for $250.

For noncore vaccines, such as Potomac Horse Fever once a year and Flu/Rhino twice a year, the vet will charge $120, but if you do it yourself it will be $43 — a $77 saving for one horse. Ten horses will save you $770.

Combining the core and the noncore vaccines will save you $75 + $77 = $152 for one horse, and $1,520 for 10 horses. Over ten years that is more than $15,000!

Tip from the Trade

I asked the owner of a large equitation stable what advice she would give to reduce vet bills. She replied, "Educate yourself so that you can handle basic, frequent problems like abscesses, simple injuries, and so on, but know the signs of infections and other serious symptoms. Understand when to get help, but don't be a horse 'hypochondriac.' If you know the professional advice will be 'soak and wait a few days' or 'do hill work,' try it first and, if things get worse, then call the vet.

"And don't be timid about calling for advice. A good vet office will be happy to talk things over with a client with a good horse-management reputation and lots of horses! Build a relationship of trust with them and they'll do the same with you."

Good advice from an experienced horsewoman!

Comparative Costs for Vaccinations

Core Vaccines

GIVEN BY	EWT & WEST NILE	RABIES	VET'S FARM CALL	TOTAL
Vet	$30	$20	$50	$100
Self	$22	$ 3	—	$ 25

Noncore Vaccines

GIVEN BY	FLU/RHINO 2X A YEAR	POTOMAC HORSE FEVER	FARM CALL	TOTAL
Vet	$25 × 2 = 50	$20	$50	$120
Self	$15 × 2 = 30	$13	—	$ 43

Antigens vs. Antibodies

Antigens are disease-causing organisms, such as tetanus bacteria. Antibodies are the structures that seek out, attack, and dispose of the antigens. The body produces antibodies to get rid of the antigens and prevent the diseases they cause.

How Vaccinations Work

Let's start with the routine herd-health areas that you may be able to do yourself.

It's helpful to understand a few of the principles of immunology, the science of developing immunity or protection against the ravages of disease. Unvaccinated, vulnerable horses have a naive immune system. This means that they have never been exposed to the disease-causing agent and, therefore, have not developed any immunity and could contract any disease to which they are exposed.

AN EPIC BATTLE

Let me explain in very basic and general terms. There is an epic battle being waged daily against your horse's health. Let's use the analogy of a fort. His body is the fort. There are "special forces" soldiers (antibodies) that have been trained to detect certain enemies, the antigens. The antibodies have been exposed to this enemy before and have learned everything about it. They have trained others in the fort to detect it. When these specialized antibodies find the antigen, they attack it and remove it from the fort. Over time, the antibody soldiers get old and die off and new ones need to be exposed and trained to detect the enemy (in the form of a booster vaccine).

When you give the primary vaccine to your horse (the first time he is ever vaccinated), you are actually giving a small dose of the disease antigen: either live, modified-live, or killed vaccine. The horse's immune system kicks in and develops antibodies that remember that particular disease antigen. When you give the second vaccine or third vaccine a few weeks later, called a "booster vaccine," it greatly multiplies the amount of antibodies ready to fight the disease. Over time, the antibodies die off and the number found in the blood, if you were to test it, would not be sufficient to fight off another attack. That's when it's time to revaccinate, usually annually, to boost the immune system.

Most vaccines require an initial injection, then a second injection (possibly a third) 2 to 4 weeks later. After that, the horse may need to be vaccinated only annually and not with the double dose it required the first time.

Degree of Exposure

How closely your horse was in contact with a sick horse is called the degree of exposure. For example, did a horse with influenza breathe on your horse as it walked by at a horse show, or were they trailered next to each other for 4 hours traveling to the show?

HOW EFFECTIVE IS VACCINATION?

Vaccinating is not a 100-percent guarantee that your horse will not contract the disease. There are many factors that contribute to immunity, including the effectiveness of the vaccine itself, the handling and administration of the vaccine, the degree of exposure of the animal to the infectious agent, the condition of the animal, his age, management practices directed at disease control, and so on. The vaccine may not prevent the horse from contracting the disease, but it should at least have less-deleterious effects than if he were not vaccinated.

Also, there is the possibility of a vaccine reaction. See page 172 for more on this.

What to Vaccinate Against and When

There are many vaccines and combinations of vaccines on the market, and it can be very confusing sifting through the products. First, let's talk about the diseases we can vaccinate horses against to help prevent disease.

Noncore Vaccinations

Noncore vaccinations include:

- Anthrax
- Botulism
- Equine Herpes Virus
- Equine Viral Arteritis
- Influenza
- Potomac Horse Fever
- Rotovirus
- Strangles

The noncore vaccines are given if there is prevalence of disease in your area or according to the use and exposure of your horse. For example, horses that are exposed to new horses may need Influenza/Rhinopnuemonitis or Strangles vaccines. Broodmares need a different series of Equine Herpes Virus vaccine than a school horse would. Teaser stallions may need Equine Viral Arteritis. If Potomac Horse Fever is a problem in your area, you need to vaccinate for that. Other areas may need to vaccinate for Anthrax, Rotovirus, and Botulism.

Contact your local veterinarian or vet school to determine which vaccines should be given in your area and for your specific farm needs. Your veterinarian can design a herd health-care program for your farm and also teach you the correct way to vaccinate your horses.

CORE VACCINATIONS

The American Association of Equine Practitioners (AAEP) puts out a guide for recommendations for equine vaccinations. In 2009, AAEP changed the recommendations for core vaccines: the group used to recommend just Eastern and Western Encephalitis and Tetanus, but now have added Rabies and West Nile Virus. This is the first revision to the recommendations in 7 years, but you can and should check online for updates, as well as for the frequency and detailed dose series.

Administering a Vaccination

You can greatly reduce your routine veterinary bills by vaccinating your own horses, but you need to have the proper equipment and learn the correct procedure.

SYRINGES AND NEEDLES

Syringes come in a variety of sizes. Vaccines for horses are usually 1 to 2 ml (or "cc"). You can buy a box of 3-cc disposable syringes with the 1.5-inch needles already attached. There are lines on the syringes that say 1, 2, or 3 cc.

Needles also come in a variety of sizes. The larger the number, the smaller the size of the bore (hole) of the needle; therefore, a 16-gauge needle has a bigger hole than a 22-gauge needle. For vaccines, 22-gauge needles are sufficient. You want a longer needle to go deep into the muscle; 1- or 1.5 inch needles are fine for intramuscular injections. The bigger the horse, the longer the needle needed. Foals can use a 1-inch needle.

READ THE VACCINE LABEL

Always read the directions on the bottle; there's lots of interesting and useful information there. Here are some things to look for.

Check the expiration date. Don't use the product if the date has passed.

What's the correct dosage? 1 cc or 2? Rabies for dogs is 1 cc, but for horses it is 2, even though a large dog may be bigger than a miniature horse.

Route of injection or administration. If it says IN (intranasal), do not inject intramuscularly. (See below for more information.)

Shake well or gently rock? Some vaccines can settle in the bottom of the vial. Read the directions, which may say shake or rock gently back and forth.

Maintain the "cold chain." Keep vaccines in the recommended temperature range. Almost all vaccines need to be refrigerated to keep the product effective. Store in the dark between 35°F and 45°F (2°C and 7°C). Do not freeze.

DEVELOP A RELIABLE SYSTEM

In case of a vaccine reaction (see page 172) I like to know which vaccine was the culprit, so I label my vaccines after I draw them up. I use a Sharpie pen and just put the initial on the end of the plunger (e.g., R = Rabies). I administer any vaccines with an R on the horse's right side and the others on the left. Rabies, Rabies/Potomac, and Flu/Rhino go on the right; EWT and WNV go on the left.

ROUTES OF INJECTION

How you inject the vaccination is called the "route" of injection or administration. The four routes are:

- **Intramuscular (IM).** Goes deep into the muscle. All of the core vaccines horses need are given IM

Keeping Cool

It is necessary to maintain the "cold chain" from the manufacturer to the horse. This means the vaccines must be kept cool from the manufacturing site to the injection site. They need to be shipped cool and placed in a refrigerator. Place them in the center of the refrigerator, not the door or back wall, where temperatures can vary.

This also means you need to have the horses up and ready to be vaccinated when you pull the vaccine out of the refrigerator. Don't have the vials sitting on the dash of your car in the August sun while you catch and tie up all of the horses. If the product becomes warm, it may lose its effect entirely or reduce the protection afforded your horses. Don't use it.

Check to make sure vaccines coming from manufacturers have remained cool during shipment.

Learn from My Mistakes

Never remove the cap from the needle with your teeth. I once removed the cap off a syringe I had drawn up with euthanasia solution. I had accidentally bumped the hub of the syringe while climbing over the fence and when I pulled the top off the needle with my teeth, I got a euthanasia solution in my mouth. Not a good thing! Nor would it be good to accidentally get vaccine in your mouth. So begin with good technique and careful habits.

- **Subcutaneous (SQ).** Injected just under the skin
- **Intravenous (IV).** Goes in the vein, usually the jugular, and should be done by the veterinarian because there is risk of injecting into the carotid artery and it going to the brain, causing seizures and, possibly, death. No vaccines are currently given in the vein
- **Intranasal (IN).** Squirted up the horse's nose

AREAS OF INJECTION

The areas suitable for IM injections in horses are the neck, hind end, and chest (pectoral muscle). I prefer the neck because I don't like to get kicked. If the horse gets really sore in the neck, I give some Banamine before the next vaccination time and administer the injection in the pectoral muscle in the chest.

Where in the neck do you inject IM vaccines? You can administer them:

- below the crest of the neck
- above the cervical vertebrae
- in front of the shoulder

These points form a nice triangle to guide you in where to inject.

PRACTICE

If you have never vaccinated before, you need to waste a few needles and syringes practicing. And if you are nervous around needles, just remember that you developed that fear because you've been on the receiving end. Now you are on the giving end and you can strive to be calm, careful, and efficient.

Buy some lemons. Fill a glass with water. Practice drawing up 1 and 2 cc of water to the line on the syringe. Inject the water into the lemon so there is no air in the syringe.

Practice drawing back and injecting quickly. The less time it takes you to vaccinate, the less chance of the horse objecting and someone getting hurt.

Safety first. If you have any doubts, call your vet to vaccinate.

PROPER VACCINATION TECHNIQUE IN NINE STEPS

When you are ready, make sure you have a good handler who can hold the horse still. Perform your first vaccinations on quiet horses. Make sure the area is clear and safe to avoid accidents if the horse jumps.

1. Fill your syringe with the proper dose and have it ready before you approach the horse.

2. Before you begin vaccinating, make friends with the horse. Talk to him or pet him. Don't just walk up and jab him in the neck; he won't like it. You may get the first needle in but not the second.

3. Do not touch the needle. It is sterile; you are not. Whatever is on your fingers you will inject into your horse, such as Staph bacteria.

4. When you remove the cap from the needle, put it where you can find it. Have a system, such as always in your right pocket, not in your mouth.

5. It is helpful to distract the horse from the pain of the injection. I am right-handed, so I push my left index finger into the horse's neck close to where I am going to inject. This seems to get the horse thinking about my finger pressure, and he doesn't seem to feel the injection as much. This also gives me some stability.

6. Stick the needle into the neck up to the hub, quickly and deftly. Do not be timid and have to stick several times. If you do, you will make your horse needle-shy and then even your vet won't want to come out and vaccinate him.

7. Once you have stuck in the needle up to the hub, quickly pull back on the plunger to aspirate any blood and see whether you are in a vessel.

8. If you see blood in the syringe, don't pull the needle all the way out. Simple pull it out slightly and redirect it, aspirate again, and then press the plunger if there is no blood. Vaccines are supposed to go IM, not IV.

9. Replace the cap immediately. Dispose of needle and syringe in a biohazard box; find out whether your vet will dispose of it for you for a fee.

Giving a Vaccination

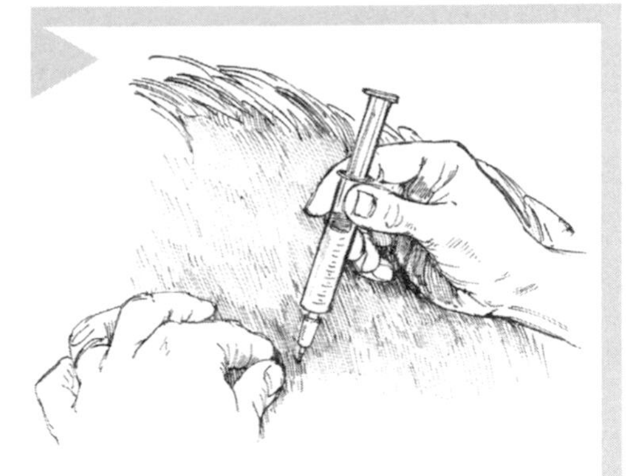

Stick the needle in up to the hub.

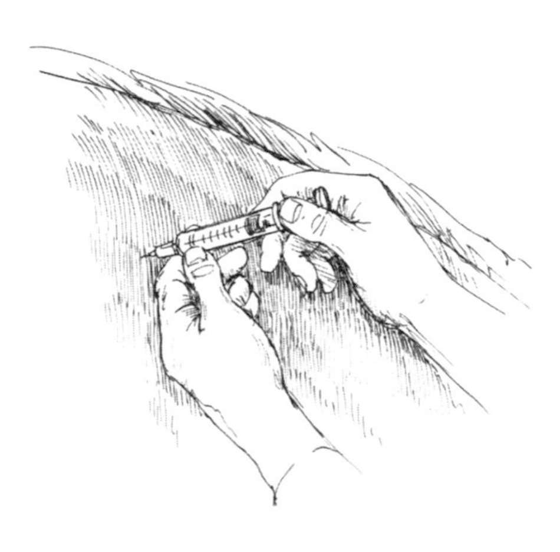

Quickly pull back on the plunger. If you aspirate any blood pull the needle partway out and redirect it. Aspirate again.

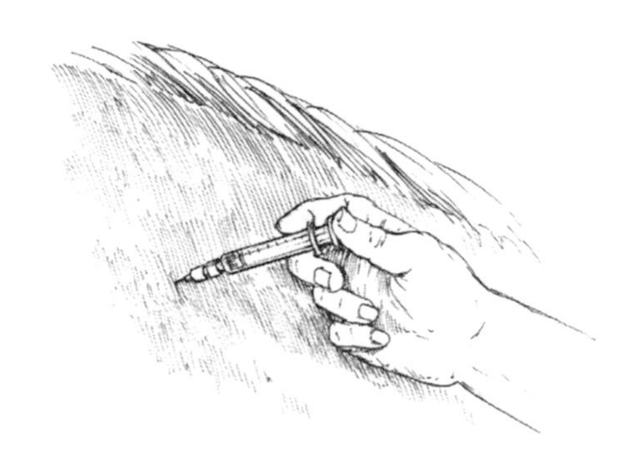

If there is no blood aspirated, press the plunger.

Turnout Can Work Wonders

If you are trying to cut costs, try some "Dr. Sunshine" and "Mr. Greengrass" to see whether pasture turnout improves the situation. This is particularly true for respiratory conditions, stocking up, stress, and boredom. Horses were not created to live inside stalls.

WHAT ARE THE RISKS?

As with most medical procedures there are some potential risks associated with vaccines. Occasionally, a horse will have a reaction to the vaccine. This can range from simple soreness to an abscess to an anaphylactic reaction and death.

Soreness

When you receive a tetanus shot, your arm may hurt for a few days. With the combination injections (many vaccines combined into one shot), your horse may receive seven vaccines in the neck and it can become quite sore. The pain can be relieved by cold-hosing the area for 15 minutes twice a day and a few days of treatment with Banamine.

Watch to make sure the neck isn't so sore that the horse doesn't want to bend down to eat or drink. If this is the case, hang hay and water off the ground.

Abscesses

Rarely, an abscess may form. This may need to be drained and, possibly, antibiotics administered. Also, you may not have obtained a good immune response. Check with your vet.

Anaphylactic Reaction

Although an anaphylactic reaction is extremely rare, always watch your horses after vaccines are given. Call your veterinarian immediately if a horse breaks out in hives and begins having an adverse reaction. The vet may come out and give epinephrine or steroids. These need to be given in a timely fashion.

What Should You Give and When?

The AAEP (American Association of Equine Practitioners) has guidelines on its Web site. Check to make sure these recommendations have not changed, and consult with your local vet to see what you need in your area beyond the core vaccines.

Core vaccines need to be given every year and are considered necessary for all horses, regardless of their use. Equine Eastern and Western Encephalitis, Tetanus, West Nile Virus, and Rabies are the current core recommendations.

ADULT HORSES

The following are suggestions; however, it is essential to check with your local vet to be sure this regimen is suited to your herd and your area of the country.

Eastern and Western Equine Encephalitis

Vaccinate annually in spring, before the vector (mosquito) season. In endemic areas (where there are many cases), consider every 6 months.

Tetanus Toxoid

Vaccinate annually. Revaccinate in case of injury if more than 6 months since last tetanus vaccination.

Tetanus Antitoxin

Different from the above tetanus toxoid, tetanus antitoxin is used if previously unvaccinated horses are injured, in order to give an immediate passive immune response.

Note: I have never used an antitoxin on a horse and I don't recommend its use. Theiler's disease is a rare, but fatal, consequence of using the tetanus antitoxin. The use of antitoxin should be determined by a veterinarian to see whether the benefits outweigh the risks. If indicated, the antitoxin should be given at one site and the initial dose of the series of tetanus toxoid vaccinations in a distant muscular site.

West Nile Virus

Vaccinate annually in spring before the beginning of the vector (mosquito) season, but give vaccinations every 6 months in endemic areas or in horses younger than 5 years or more than 15 years old. The cases of West Nile disease in horses are down; however, this is because so many people are vaccinating their horses, not because it is no longer exists, so it vaccinations are still recommended.

Getting It Right

Here are four vaccination essentials to remember.

1. **Develop a Plan with your Vet** You must tailor your vaccination program to your herd and your location with the help of a licensed professional.
2. **Stay Tuned to the AAEP** Research updates the protocol, so do not proceed without first checking the AAEP Web site for the latest recommendations.
3. **Read the Label** Never forget to scrutinize the vial label for injection route, amount of dosage, frequency, and expiration.
4. **Keep Good Records** Don't waste vaccine dollars by revaccinating a horse that has already been vaccinated, or by vaccinating earlier than necessary, simply because you didn't write it down.

Promote Herd Immunity

Vaccinate all of the horses in the herd at the same time. That way, if some of the horses don't mount as an effective response to the vaccine as others, they may still be protected. Because the entire herd has immunity, the chance of this horse catching the disease is reduced.

Tailor your herd-health program to save money without sacrificing protection. Not all horses need every vaccine available to them. You need to think through what vaccines you really need to be giving each horse.

This includes Coggins tests for Equine Infectious Anemia. If you have some old horses on your place that never leave the farm, they won't need a Coggins and probably not many of the other vaccines either.

Rabies

Vaccinate adults annually. Rabies is zoonotic, which means humans can get it if exposed to a rabid horse, so I recommend giving the rabies vaccine, particularly if you run a riding stable.

FOAL VACCINES

All core vaccines except West Nile Virus require a three-dose initial series with the first at 4 to 6 months old, the second 4 to 6 weeks after the first, and the third at 10 to 12 months.

With foals from an unvaccinated broodmare, the core vaccine series starts at 3 to 4 months, tetanus at 1 to 4 months, then every 4 weeks with a series.

West Nile Virus

From nonvaccinated mares, start at 3 months or younger; others, still give at 5 to 6 months. In the southeastern United States, foals begin the series at 3 months. Read directions specific for different types of the West Nile vaccine and the age requirements.

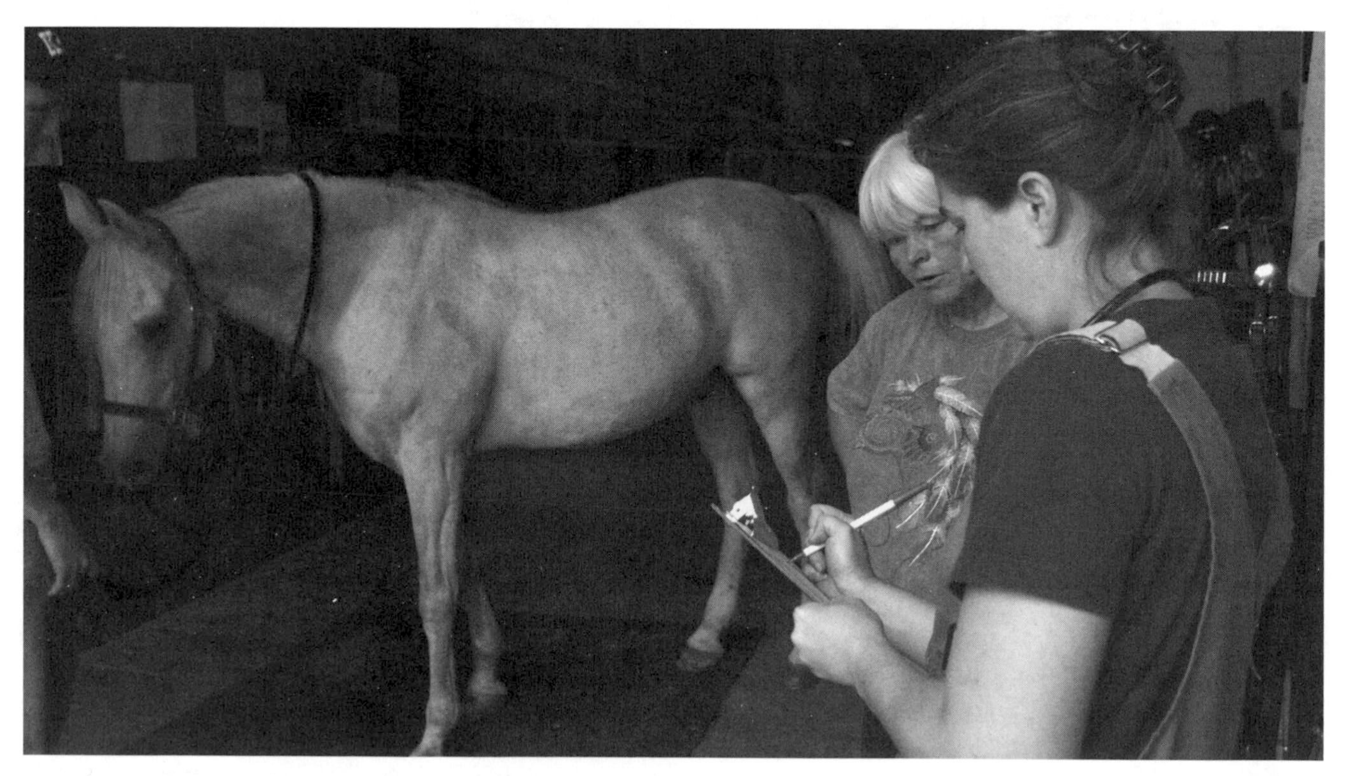

Keeping accurate records is vital to your health-care program.

Rabies, Influenza and Strangles

Series of three beginning at 6 months.

BROODMARES

Consult with your vet to design a vaccine program for your breeding herd. Vaccinating a broodmare is complicated because you must protect the pregnancy and the foal. Give core vaccines and EIV/EHV (influenza and herpes inactivated) 1 and 4 at 4 to 6 weeks before foaling.

Rhinopneumonitis, Equine Herpes Virus (EHV)

Give three vaccines at 5, 7, and 9 months of gestation, using only vaccines labeled for protection against abortion (Pneumabort K and Prodigy). Check with your vet.

Rotavirus

Give three vaccines at 8, 9, and 10 months. Mares naïve to viral diseases will not respond to viral vaccines while pregnant. Depending on the area, one may not be necessary. Again, check with your vet.

BACKYARD HORSES

Previously vaccinated horses should receive annual vaccinations for Eastern and Western Encephalitis (EEE and WEE), West Nile Virus, Tetanus, Rabies, Influenza, and Herpes. If there is a prolonged mosquito season, then vaccinate twice a year for EEE, WEE, and West Nile Virus.

PERFORMANCE HORSES

If they were previously vaccinated, performance horses that travel need the core vaccines annually. Give Eastern and Western Encephalitis and Tetanus, West Nile Virus, and Rabies annually; Influenza and EHV semiannually; and Strangles *(Streptococcus equi)* annually or semiannually. Vaccination is not recommended in the face of an outbreak of Strangles.

Tell your vet where you are traveling with your horses; she may recommend other vaccines.

Strangles Alert

If you are giving the Strangles (streptococcus) vaccine, do it last and use gloves. If you get the vaccine on your hands and then pat the next horse on the neck before you vaccinate it, you may vaccinate through the strep and an abscess could develop.

Dewormer cost for one year for one horse given every 2 months

Here's the difference in cost between the vet making a farm call and administering dewormer, and you doing it yourself.

	VET	SELF
EQUIMAX farm call	$25 + $50 $75	$14
IVERMECTIN farm call #1	$15 + $50 $65	$ 3
IVERMECTIN farm call #2	$15 + $50 $65	$ 3
IVERMECTIN farm call #3	$15 + $50 $65	$ 3
IVERMECTIN farm call #4	$15 + $50 $65	$ 3
IVERMECTIN farm call #5	$15 + $50 $65	$ 3
IVERMECTIN farm call #6	$15 + $50 $65	$ 3
TOTAL	$465	$32

Do-It-Yourself Deworming

Now that you know how to vaccinate your own horses, the next preventive measure you need to take for good horse health is to deworm your horses. Usually it is even simpler than vaccinating. So why deworm your horse yourself instead of paying the vet?

Say you have done fecal exams and the vet has determined a year-long plan for your farm. He has decided that you need to deworm every 2 months since you have a high concentration of young horses on a small paddock.

How much will that cost you?

- If you have the vet come out to deworm one horse every 2 months for a year it will cost you $465.
- If you do one horse yourself it will cost you $32.
- Ten horses done by the vet will cost you $4,650.
- Ten horses dewormed by you will cost $320.
- Ten horses for ten years by the vet costs $46,500 compared to $3,200 by you.

Obviously this will vary with the frequency and dewormer needed, but it is clear that you will save significantly if you deworm your own horses.

Parasites 101

Now that you are convinced that you should deworm your horses yourself, you need to know some of the basics of parasitology, the science of parasites. There are more than 150 different parasites that can infest horses, but the most important ones to worry about can be counted on one hand. There are also a variety of different dewormers on the market; however, the active ingredients can also be counted on one hand.

It can be confusing to figure out what product to use to deworm for which parasite, and when and why deworm at all. And are there other ways to control parasites other than antiparasiticals? The following explanation should be helpful.

WHY DEWORM?

Parasites are extremely undesirable. They cause:

- Less than optimal performance
- More grain must be fed with less results

- Dull, shaggy coat
- Colic
- Rarely, death (especially in young horses)

This is why it is essential to deworm your horses.

MONEY-SAVING TIP

One vet call for a mild colic case will cost more than a good year of deworming!

HOW OFTEN?

This depends on many factors: stocking ratio (the number of horses per acre), age, pasture maintenance and, most importantly, parasite load.

You will need to deworm more often if you have:

- a densely populated pasture (10 horses per acre instead of the optimal one horse per 10 acres)
- young or old horses
- broodmares
- poor manure removal

I do not recommend the daily dewormer because it is expensive and there is evidence that it has contributed to the growing resistance in parasites.

WHAT PRODUCT SHOULD BE USED?

Take the time to educate yourself about what products to use for which worms.

Stomach bots. Only Ivermectin and Moxidectin kill these, so typically use after the first frost once a year in the colder climates.

Tapeworms. Praziquantel or a large dose of pyrantel are the only ones that kill "tapes," which have been found to cause colic. Use twice a year. It is usually combined with Ivermectin in products like Equimax and Zimectrin Gold.

Encysted strongyles. Sometimes with a horse that is debilitated or has frequent bouts of colic, the cause may be encysted worms that migrate. This is not usually a big problem in horses. Options, in order of least to most expensive, are Fenbendazole, Moxidectin, and the Pancacur Power Pack.

All of the other equine parasites of importance are killed by Ivermectin, Fenbendazole, Albendazole, Benzimidizole, and Moxidectin.

Look for the Active Ingredient

The key element in a dewormer is the active ingredient. If the active ingredient is 1.87 percent Ivermectin, then no matter what the brand name says, it is Ivermectin; don't pay more for fancy packaging and marketing. The generic Ivermectin is the same thing.

Terminology to Know

Fecal count. When you take a sample of the feces of a horse to the vet office, they'll look under the microscope and count the eggs that the parasite has released into the feces. This gives an indication of the parasite load in the horse. (Tapeworm eggs are not able to be counted this way, so we routinely deworm for tapes twice a year.) Deworming based on the fecal count results gives you an informed decision on which horses need what and how often. Ideally, you should take a sample 2 weeks after you deworm to see if there is resistance to the dewormer and to determine when to deworm next. This may be impractical with a large herd, and you can just take a sampling. Then spot-check one or two times a year. Develop a plan with your vet for fecal sampling.

Resistance. A dewormer will kill most of the parasites, but if the correct dosage is not used, the tougher ones survive and develop resistance to the dewormers. The next generation of worms not killed by the dewormer is more resistant. As more and more resistant parasites develop, soon the parasites are so resistant that the dewormer has little effect on them at all.

Herd plan. Have your vet make a recommendation for your herd specifying which dewormers are really necessary.

Alternative dewormer. Alternatives to using dewormers to control parasites include: picking up manure, not feeding on the ground, pasture rotation, and reducing the stocking number of horses per pasture.

Designing and implementing a sound parasite management plan for horses and pastures reduces the parasite load and saves money on dewormers.

HOW TO DEWORM IN SIX STEPS

1. Read the directions on the product.
2. Have your horse tied up so he is not eating anything. I have seen many horses spit out the dewormer in the wad of grass they were chewing.
3. Weigh your horse with a weight tape. It is better to be slightly over the dosage then under, because giving an inadequate amount of dewormer helps to develop resistant parasites.
4. Move the dial on the plunger to the correct weight and remove the top. (A panicked client called me one day and said she was deworming her horse, and she pushed and pushed the plunger. Then she heard a pop and into the horse went the dewormer, plastic top and all. She asked if it would hurt the horse. I said it would probably pass through, but it was much easier to get the dewormer out with the top removed!)
5. Using the correct labeled dosage, place the nozzle against the inside back of the cheek, not directly on the tongue and send the plunger home.
6. Wash your hands or face or whatever body part the horse has smeared the white paste on. It can be absorbed and end up deworming you!

Coping with Emergencies

When do you call the vet? Farm calls can cost anywhere from $50 to $125 depending on your area. This is before the vet even gets out of the truck.

How do you know when it is really necessary to call the vet? Take a deep breath and assess the situation. Sometimes it is just our nerves, and sometimes there is a gut intuition that matters are serious enough to call the vet.

If you are unsure and worried about any condition, call the vet.

If the horse's value and future are hindered in any way by the condition, call the vet.

When you call, ask the vet whether it is really necessary for her to come out or if she can monitor the condition over the phone.

Resistance

I asked Dr. Anne Zajac, the parasitologist at Virginia Maryland College of Veterinary Medicine, for the latest insights on equine parasite control and she said:

"The forefront of knowledge of equine parasitology is in a state of flux due to the increasing resistance to the antiparasiticals on the market. The best thing to do is to ask your veterinarian what the current recommendations are. Horse owners need to be thinking of better alternatives to using dewormers, such as grazing exposure and manure removal.

"The practice of deworming every horse with a different dewormer every two months is no longer considered good management. Fecal testing enables you to make informed decisions to deworm the heavy egg shedders in the herd more than those with a lower fecal egg count.

"If horse owners do not begin to make wise decisions regarding the use of dewormers, there will be so much resistance to dewormers that there will be no effective product left on the market. There is only one new dewormer that is currently being researched but it will not be in the United States for many years. When it arrives, if good management is not used, then that will soon be ineffective as well."

Good advice. Let us as vets and horse owners do all that we can to reduce the development of resistance.

Trailer Tips

Trailers and trailering can be implicated in a variety of injuries. I was called to sew up a large head laceration on a horse. When I lifted up the torn skin flap there was yellow paint on the horse's skull bone. I asked if the inside of the trailer was yellow and they said "yes"! This could have been prevented if the horse had worn a head bumper attached to the halter.

Catastrophic trailering injuries, such as floors falling out and doors flying open on the highway, can be prevented with good trailer and vehicular maintenance. Many injuries in people and horses occur because horses are not properly trained to load on a trailer and get scared and beaten on. Take the time to train the horse to load and unload; it saves money in the long run.

The following are suggestions on saving on vet bills and how to treat some common conditions yourself. You may, however, miss something a trained veterinarian would catch and delay the healing or exacerbate it. So my disclaimer is to call the vet if there is any doubt.

COMMON EMERGENCY SITUATIONS

The following are the most frequent vet calls I receive as an equine practitioner, with suggestions on how you can cope and when to seek professional intervention.

LAMENESS AND STIFFNESS

What you can do. If the area feels hot, rest the leg and cold-hose the area, 15 minutes twice a day. Give some anti-inflammatories, such as Phenylbutazone (Bute) or Flunixin Meglamin (Banamine), according to the label directions, or a less ulcergenic anti-inflammatory such as Fibroxx. I like Bute for bones and Banamine for soft tissue pain. Much lameness is the result of rough-housing in the pasture or overstrenuous training, and rest and some anti-inflammatories will take care of the problem without spending the money to have the vet come out. You may save yourself $150 by trying these things first.

When to call the vet. If the lameness worsens or does not clear up in 2 weeks, call the vet. She can localize the lameness with nerve blocks and take radiographs. If you aren't in any big hurry to get to a show, why don't you save the initial vet charge?

LACERATIONS

You have just pulled your horse in from the pasture, and he has a big gash on his neck. To suture or not to suture?

What you can do. If you apply pressure to stop the bleeding, hose it, and bandage the wound, will it do just fine? Does it really need an antibiotic? Can you give some penicillin or Trimethoprim Sulfate? Can you manage the scar tissue (proud flesh) with some proud flesh ointment? Do you need to booster the tetanus? You can do that yourself.

When to call the vet. Your vet can help you evaluate the situation over the phone. If the wound is near or in a joint or tendon, call the vet. If he is an expensive show horse, call the vet. If he is a school horse, however, will it matter if it heals on its own and leaves a slightly bigger scar?

Prevention. Prevent lacerations by combing fence lines and barns for stray bits of wire or nails. Prevent trailer injuries by using head bumpers and leg bandages and by making sure your trailer and truck are in top condition.

ABSCESSES AND FRACTURES

What you can do. My boss used to say, "If a horse is three-legged lame, it is either a hoof abscess or a fracture." Before you call the vet, pick up the foot. I've been called out for a lameness call, and the horse had a big stone wedged between the frog and shoe.

The majority of lameness occurs in the foot. If you suspect an abscess, use hoof testers to locate the area of pain and, if you are skilled with a hoof knife, pare out the sore spot until you find a pocket of pus or soak it until it softens and then pare it out. Have your vet show you how to do this the first time, and when you feel confident, do it yourself.

Is the horse current on his tetanus? If not, he will need a booster.

"What Can't I Do Myself?"

The question to ask yourself is what could the vet do that I can't do myself? If you have a well-stocked first-aid box, can you treat the condition yourself?

These are broad generalizations, so take them as such and use your head. Don't be a horse hypochondriac; it is expensive — but also don't take risks that make you uncomfortable.

Wild horses make it on their own without the aid of a veterinarian; sometimes as owners we can be too quick to call. Your horse's value and use and your pocketbook may determine whether you need to call the vet or your horse should go for surgery.

Comparing one leg to the other will often make evident the swelling on the lame one.

Alternative Treatments and Supplements

Some people swear by acupuncture, massage, chiropractics, and supplements, and if you are in a performance-type situation where any edge may make the difference and you can afford it, go for it. If it is a school horse, on the other hand, one month of rest may give the same results and be much less expensive than a month of acupuncture, massages, chiropractics, and supplements. I am skeptical when it is hard to tell definitively whether it is the treatment or the time off that helps the condition.

The same goes for the various joint, hoof, and performance supplements that are being fed to horses today in unprecedented quantities. Many of these have no scientific proof of being effective and may even be harmful (even some sold by vets). Remember, everything you read online is not based on sound scientific research; some products are simply voodoo potions. If a supplement doesn't have FDA approval, don't use it.

Often the tract will pop out at the coronary band. Push around the top of the hoof and see whether it is painful or you see a draining area. Once the pressure is relieved, the pain subsides. Putting some iodine in and wrapping to keep it clean for a week or so is a good idea, although some say once the track is opened it will heal without additional treatment.

Foot abscesses can take up to 6 weeks to come out. If your farrier is scheduled to come to the farm, have him pare it out for you. He is already there and is less expensive than your vet.

COLD/RUNNY NOSE

What you can do. What would the vet do? Check the temperature and the lymph nodes. If the lymph nodes under the jaw aren't swollen and it isn't strangles, it is probably some strain of influenza. You shouldn't put your horse on antibiotics because they treat only bacterial infections, not flu viruses.

Is your horse eating and drinking? Even if he has a high temperature (more than 102°F), the vet can't really do anything but give some Banamine to keep the fever down or, if it is very early in the disease process, some of the new (expensive) antiviral medication.

Separate the horse from other horses so that the infection doesn't go through the barn. Hose him down or give alcohol baths if his temperature gets too high.

If your horse develops a secondary bacterial infection, he may need antibiotics. Yellow mucus running out the nose is not necessarily a bacterial infection; however, at this point, most owners will panic and call the vet. If you have Trimethoprim Sulfate in your medicine cabinet, ask your vet whether you can give that or run by the office and pick some up. This will save you the farm call and treatment charge.

When to call the vet. If the horse is having trouble breathing or is off his feed and you are worried, call the vet. The vet can listen to the lungs to check for pneumonia. Most runny noses, however, clear up on their own in a week.

Top 10 Ways to Reduce Vet Bills

In addition to doing your own vaccinating and deworming, there are other things that, with some education and a healthy respect for "when to call the vet," you can do yourself. You'll save hundreds of dollars in vet bills, not to mention $100,000 to $250,000 for vet school tuition!

1. **Quality feed saves on colic calls and prevents poor nutrition.**
2. **Water must be clean and fresh.** Heating the winter water supply so horses drink more water can avoid impaction colics.
3. **Lock feed rooms so there is no grain overload and subsequent founder.** This also keeps out opossums, a potential source for Equine Protozoal Myeloencephalitis.
4. **Regular farrier work by a qualified blacksmith saves on lameness and lay-up time.**
5. **Active maintenance of fences and pastures prevents wire cuts, toxic plants, and eye ulcers.**
6. **Make sure not to park equipment in the pastures with the horses.** I've seen tragedies involving hay balers, fertilizer spreaders, and more. If horses can get into trouble, they will. Park equipment outside of the pastures.
7. **Exercise biosecurity management by quarantining incoming horses.**
8. **Cockle burrs in the forelock are the main cause of eye ulcers.** Remove them from your pasture.
9. **Don't overfloat your horse's teeth.**
10. **Educate yourself with good veterinary books and learn from your veterinarian and other experienced horsemen.**

COLIC

Colic is the Number 1 emergency vet call. Ninety percent of colic cases do not need surgery. That's the good news. Since 10 percent do need surgery or they will die, you need to determine ahead of time whether you are willing to spend the money to take a horse to surgery. When the vet asks you the question, it can be a very emotional moment and not a time when sound business judgment prevails. (See the sidebar on page 186.)

The odds are in your favor that your horse doesn't need to go for surgery.

What you can do. Do a physical exam (see How to Examine a Horse on page 185). Call your vet and tell her the results of your exam. Also tell her that you have Banamine

What Vets Do for Colic

I have had many colic calls where the panicked owner called because the horse did not finish his grain. My boss said, "Never miss the chance to tube and palpate a colic call." When the vet comes out to your farm, we can only rely on what you have said — that the horse was showing signs of pain and was not eating — so we assume it is colicky and tube with mineral oil and usually some electrolytes even if the physical exam is fairly unremarkable. The horse may not have really needed it, but it makes the owner feel better.

Vets have been giving mineral oil for years, but does it really do that much? Most vets, if they are going out after hours for a colic call, are going to do something so they don't get called back at 3:00 in the morning.

and are going to give it orally — and do so. You must reduce the pain and get whatever is causing it to move on through the gastrointestinal tract.

Remove all feed and hay.

If you want to walk the horse you can, but not to the point of exhaustion. You can walk him to keep him from rolling and twisting an intestine or getting all banged up. But if he will lie down quietly, that's okay.

Can you give Banamine and wait to see whether the horse improves without having the vet come out?

In winter many horses get impactions because the water is so cold they don't want to drink it. The dehydration, along with the dry hay, makes a painful impaction, like constipation — painful but rarely fatal.

Some horses get very painful gas colic and go down. Sometimes trotting them out and letting them pass the gas relieves the pain and they are better before the vet even arrives.

When to call the vet. If you or your vet has any suspicion that your horse may be a surgical candidate, get the vet out to your farm or take the horse into the vet school or wherever they are going to do surgery. The sooner the better because the longer you wait, the more compromised the gut will become and the poorer the prognosis.

Prevention. Practice colic prevention management:

- Lock feed rooms.
- Check water quantity and temperature.
- Change rations gradually.
- Don't buy cribbers or horses with a history of colic or surgery.
- Reduce stress.
- Feed more roughage and less grain.
- Keep horses outside and exercise them regularly.

ULCERS

Some colic is caused by ulcers. Equine ulcers affect up to 90 percent of racehorses and 60 percent of show horses. A horse's stomach continuously secretes acid because equines are made to graze outside and have a regular intake of roughage throughout the day. We put them in stalls and feed them twice a day, which can lead to ulcers.

How to Examine a Horse

Ask your vet to teach you how to do a physical exam. Here are some simple things to look, listen, and feel for.

- Take the heart rate, temperature, and respiratory rate for each horse when he is healthy, so you know what is normal. Write this information down and keep it with the horse's health record.
- Learn to listen for gut sounds. Sound is good; no sound is not so good.
- Check the color of the gums and the "capillary refill" time. Capillary refill time is how quickly the pink color returns to the gums after you press your finger into them and they blanch white. Less than 2 seconds is normal.

The other thing that can cause ulcers in horses is administration of nonsteroidal, anti-inflammatory drugs like Bute, which decreases the protective mucus-producing layer in the horse's stomach. There are now some nonsteroidal anti-inflammatory drugs on the market, such as Fibroxx, which don't produce ulcers.

The major symptom is a recurring colic. Other signs could be decreased performance, and poor appetite and hair coat. The only way to diagnose an ulcer is by using an endoscope to actually look at the stomach lining with a light and camera. The most effective treatment for ulcers is Gastrogard (omeprazole), which is very expensive, especially when added to the cost of colic calls, endoscope, and loss of performance.

Keep hay in front of them in the stalls; this buffers the stomach acid. Reduce grain, which forms volatile fatty acids. Ulcers are a human-made condition in horses that you can usually prevent with good management.

Compare costs. If you and your vet suspect an ulcer, what is the cost of a treatment of Omeprazole versus vet bill, endoscope, and then a treatment with Omeprazole? (Try buying directly online to save.) Or, can you just turn the horse out and reduce the stress in his environment and see whether he improves?

Preparing for a Hard Decision

If you are going to stay in the horse business, sometimes you need to make hard decisions, because if you go bankrupt it doesn't help the horses anyway. Are you going to spend $10,000 to $15,000 on surgery for that 17-year-old school horse that may get adhesions and need surgery again?

If you think you will want surgery, check into getting medical insurance so that, when the time comes, you are ready. Decide on a horse-by-horse basis if you can afford a major medical expense or will need to elect euthanasia.

Don't forget to call the insurance company to get their approval before surgery or euthanasia or they may not pay.

Also decide in advance how much you would be willing to spend for the hospital stay. If you send the horse to a referral hospital you need to tell them up front that you have a $3,000 limit (or whatever) so they don't call you a week later with a $10,000 bill.

EYES

Eye problems can be either an emergency leading to blindness or something you can treat yourself. They can be difficult to evaluate so, when in doubt, call the vet.

Abrasion, Ulcer, or Uveitis

What you can do. For red eye from trauma, conjunctivitis, or uveitis, flush with saline, apply antibiotic eye ointment, and give anti-inflammatories like Banamine orally. Eyelid swelling could be from lid trauma, conjunctivitis, or Uveitis. Apply ice, flush with saline, and give anti-inflammatories like Banamine orally.

Warning: Always check the antibiotic eye ointment to make sure it does not contain a steroid such as dexamethazone or hydrocortisone. These could delay healing and cause a minor eye problem to become a sight-threatening condition.

When to call the vet. Definitely call the vet right away if the outside surface, the cornea, is cloudy, white, or bluish. This could be a corneal ulcer, abrasion, or uveitis. Corneal ulcers left untreated in horses can deteriorate pretty quickly, resulting in a melting ulcer and blindness. Constricted pupil or squinting may be caused from pain from an ulcer, abrasion, or uveitis. Call the vet for advice. For cloudy or clear discharge, flush with saline and apply antibiotic eye ointment. Call vet if there is no improvement by the next day.

Prevention. Prevent eye problems by careful management:

- Check fences and barns for loose nails and wire. Your horses could catch and tear an eyelid on them.
- Don't stick a hay net in front of your horse for hours in a horse trailer that is bouncing along country roads. The rough hay can cause an ulcer or fill his eyes with dust.
- Remove any cocklebur plants from your pasture and any burs from his forelock. This is the number one cause of corneal scratches, leading to eye ulcers in horses.

In conclusion, if you feel confident enough and can do some of these treatments yourself, or feel more at ease after a brief phone consultation with your vet, you can save hundreds of dollars a year.

CUTTING COSTS WITHOUT CUTTING CORNERS

As the final chapter of this book unfolds, let me remind you that in order to have a successful business, you must not only generate an income from your various endeavors but you must also cut unnecessary costs. Use the following to review your management practices and see if there are ways you can streamline and cut unnecessary costs.

Feeding

When a rancher reviews the monthly feed bills, the meaning of "don't eat like a horse" becomes crystal clear. Feeding horses is no small undertaking, especially considering the dollars involved. If you're in the business to show a profit, it's important to reduce these costs as much as possible.

Getting the Ration Right

There is an epidemic of overweight pets in this country. Not only do overweight horses needlessly increase your feed bill, but by stressing their bones and joints, they may increase your veterinary bill as well.

You can experiment by gradually reducing the grain you are feeding or introducing a less-expensive feed source, and see whether your horses keep their condition. Also try combining less expensive oats to your grain mixture, up to half the ration, and observe whether your horse maintains his condition.

Develop a system for keeping track of your horses' diets and special needs.

Consider culling horses that don't earn their keep. Retired or lame horses consume valuable time, resources, and space. Find them good homes elsewhere, where they will be useful and appreciated. Gentle horses retired from your school because of age might be a welcome addition to a therapeutic-riding program. A horse with too many problems for three-day eventing may be sound enough for the local mounted police unit. Many veterinary schools would welcome the donation of a horse for research that could ultimately help all horses. Remember that it costs just as much or more to feed an unproductive horse as it does one that is making you money.

REDUCE FEED WASTE

Following are some other ways to save on feed.

Shelter the feed from the weather. Use hayracks to keep hay dry and feed bins to protect grain. Purchase smaller quantities in summer, when insects and humidity increase spoilage.

Screen and lock the feed room. This keeps out eight-, four-, and two-legged pests. In Texas, I've seen fire ants carry off a quarter of a bale of alfalfa in one night.

Routinely deworm all horses. This helps prevent internal parasites that reduce digestive efficiency, rob nutrients, cause colic, and increase the amount of feed necessary to keep a horse at its desired weight. (See chapter 12 for more on reducing veterinary costs.)

Regularly have each horse's teeth floated, or filed, to remove the points and hooks that form. As horses age, their teeth form sharp points that can cut into their gums. This can result in improper chewing, feed dribbling, and inefficient digestion. Annual veterinary examinations and floating will prevent this problem.

Balance rations. Don't underfeed or overfeed your horses. Keep a keen eye on each horse's condition and adjust the amount of feed as necessary. Mature, idle horses may need only grass or hay. Don't spend money on grain if it's not necessary. Stabled horses performing light work may do well only on grass hay or a flake of alfalfa with a flake of grass hay.

Have your hay analyzed to determine its nutrient content and how much is necessary to feed each horse. Contact your local extension agent or an agricultural college for help.

Don't buy unnecessary supplements and conditioners. A normal horse needs only a balanced ration calculated for his weight and work level. Unless he has been diagnosed with a nutritional deficiency or is performing extremely stressful work, supplements and conditioners are unnecessary. Many supplemental products are not backed by research demonstrating that they are beneficial and may even have toxic levels of some ingredients. If you must try the latest supplement fad, try the least expensive version first.

MONEY-SAVING TIP

Feed prices can fluctuate quite a bit. If one brand goes up a lot in price, be sure to check around because other brands with the same ingredients may not have changed. Be careful, however, in switching over and phasing in a new brand. Make gradual changes slowly to avoid digestive problems.

TIPS AND TRICKS

The manager of Harmony Hills Equestrian Center, an experienced horsewoman, suggests blanketing your horse in cold weather (near freezing, or higher if raining). Don't waste labor on blanketing when it really isn't very cold outside, but when the temperatures drop or there is a cold, driving rain, the added warmth will save you money. "Cold equals eating," she points out, "and eating means raising the hay cost, just to stay warm. It requires work to put blankets on and take them off as needed, but with cold weather it can save.

"Don't clip until spring," she adds, "if you need to do it at all. Their coats save money too and are healthier for them. It takes longer for them to cool down, but it is better for them overall and helps save on the feed bill, too."

Feed hay that is higher in roughage and not so high in energy. You can get clean, lower-calorie hay that is healthy, costs less, and is far better for all those easy keepers. Better to feed lots of cheaper, clean, first-cutting hay than "high test" hay. Even my harder keepers do better with this type of hay and some grain than with high-calorie hay with less roughage and greater risk for colic. Always supplement with a basic trace mineral–salt block.

Feeding hay off the ground reduces loss in the muck and decreases parasite transmission.

Keeping an Eye on Things

Avoid overfeeding! Many horses do very well with *no* grain or just enough to bring them in for daily health checks. And watch what grain you use. If you are not doing higher level

Costly Bad Habits

Horses with bad habits can be costly investments. Horses that crib, for instance, can damage expensive wooden fencing and stall doors. Horses that weave back and forth when in a stall may be predisposed to leg stress.

work with your animal, and his weight is fine, you don't need costly super-athlete feed.

If your horse has trouble maintaining his weight and you are feeding a good-quality grain two to three times a day along with free-choice hay or pasture, start looking for causes — ulcers, worms, stress, teeth problems, and so on. Treating the causes will cost a bit, but even treating ulcers pays off in lower feed and vet bills in the long run.

On our farm, we have struggled for years to keep weight on a number of Thoroughbreds. As soon as we bit the bullet and treated for ulcers, the weight quickly came on. We were soon able to feed them like "regular" horses and eliminate weight-building supplements, weight-building grains in large volumes, and other expensive treatments.

TEN WAYS TO SAVE ON PURCHASING FEED

1. Buy in bulk. Purchase a large feed bin. It will pay for itself in savings because buying larger quantities of feed is less expensive than buying individually wrapped bags.

2. Depending on the size and strength of your barn help, you may want to buy smaller, lighter bales.

3. Purchase directly from the feed source whenever possible; it's less expensive than buying from the feed store. But check the quality of any product you buy.

4. When possible, buy hay from a farmer when it is in season, and store it in a dry place for the winter months.

5. Hay can also be purchased for less if you gather it from the field yourself, saving handling costs.

6. Buy hay by weight, not by the bale. Not all bales weigh the same.

7. Sometimes the same product you buy for horses is sold for less when marketed for cattle. A farmer might try to charge a horse owner more than he would a cattle farmer for the same hay.

8. The more commercially prepared the feed product, the more expensive it will be. For example, pelleted feeds cost more than whole oats and corn.

9. Corn oil may make the coat shiny, but so does brushing. If you want to feed an oil, go to a fast-food restaurant and ask for used peanut oil.

10. Make full use of your pasture. Perform a cost analysis to see whether it would be more economical to produce your own hay and grains instead of buying them. (See chapter 11 for more information on how to do this.)

Put Your Best Hoof Forward

Try to avoid purchasing or keeping horses with chronic hoof problems. The expense for corrective shoeing, veterinary bills, loss of use, and the time you put in managing these horses quickly adds up.

Shoeing and Trims

Thousands of dollars are spent annually on shoeing. It is well worth the time to review your shoeing needs and costs to see whether there is any way to reduce expenditures. Do not, for example, automatically have every horse trimmed every so many weeks. Hoof growth varies with each horse, much in the same way that people's nails grow at different rates. Have each horse trimmed and shod according to individual needs.

Do not automatically shoe all horses. Some horses and most ponies don't need shoes at all, or need them only on the front feet. An advantage of leaving shoes off the hind hooves, when possible, is that horses are less likely to cause serious damage if they kick another horse during turnout. Use clips, calks, pads, or corrections only when absolutely necessary.

Finally, if you have a barn full of boarders that are providing your farrier with a good business, ask for a discount for shoeing your school horses. If you have to hold the boarders' horses while the blacksmith puts on shoes, charge for this service. See the Shoeing Record in appendix B, page 197, which can keep you organized concerning foot-care needs. It also will enable your boarders to know when their horses were last shod, and it provides a record to use for billing.

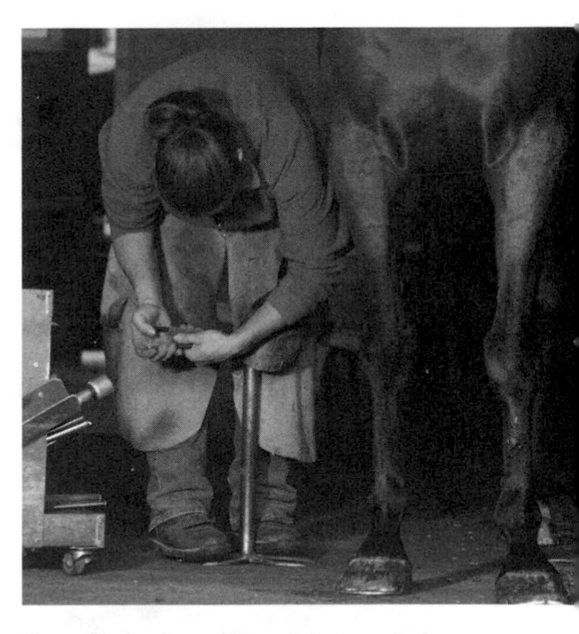

Have the farrier service your boarders on a regular schedule and ask for a discount for shoeing your school horses.

Protecting Your Investment

Protecting horses on your farm from getting out and becoming lost or stolen is an important part of their care. If the horses are insured, you or a boarder can probably recover economically, but the personal loss often is more painful.

To prevent a horse from getting lost, routinely check the locks on gates and stalls. Check on horses daily to make sure they are all accounted for so that you can take action immediately if one is missing. Quick action will increase the likelihood that the horse can be recovered quickly and safely.

Need Help?

There are organizations that provide identification record-keeping systems and that also assist in theft cases. Check horse magazines and with your veterinarian for more information. If you have registered horses, contact your breed registry for more information.

LOCATING A MISSING HORSE

If a horse turns up missing, report the loss right away to law enforcement officials. Local owners and neighbors should be contacted in case they saw anything that might help locate the horse. Ask them to help with a search effort. Initiate a telephone campaign to livestock markets and to horse auctioneers in the region. (Your local market can put you in touch with statewide and national market contacts.) These businesses are just as interested as you are in preventing the sale of stolen animals.

Direct particular attention at horse auctions scheduled 1 or 2 days after the theft. Ask horse traders, particularly those who specialize in handling horses going to the killers, to be on the lookout.

If you have a computer, put out a call for help to contacts over the Internet.

IDENTIFICATION SYSTEM

A good identification and record system for each horse is invaluable for reporting and locating lost or stolen horses. It also is necessary for insurance purposes.

Age, sex, color patterns, photographs, lip tattoos, pictures or "fingerprints" of chestnuts, electronic chips, muscular dimples, hair swirls, and scars and/or brands may be used for records and identification.

Euthanasia

Whether to bring an animal's life to an end is an unpleasant decision for anyone, but it's an important topic that must be addressed. Euthanasia may be the kindest option for any animal that is suffering because of a serious injury or illness, especially if there is no hope of recovery, or for animals that have become seriously and irreversibly debilitated because of age. Your veterinarian can help you or your client make the decision and provide information about burial, removal, or other alternatives when a horse is euthanized (or dies of natural causes).

You can obtain more information on euthanasia from a brochure developed by the American Veterinary Medical Association; your veterinarian should have copies available.

Appendixes

APPENDIXES

The forms in this section are intended to serve as examples. You are welcome to photocopy and use them; however, check first with your lawyer or accountant, as appropriate, to make sure they are suitable for your business.

APPENDIX A

Boarder Information

Owner's name: ____

Address: ____

Phone: (h) ______________ (w) ______________ (c) ______________

Emergency contact: ____

Phone: (h) ______________ (w) ______________ (c) ______________

Horse's name: ________________________ Date of birth: ______________

Breed: ____________________________ Color: ______________

Markings: ________________________

Date of arrival: ______________________ Date of departure: ______________

Veterinarian

1st choice: ______________________________ Phone: ______________

2nd choice: ______________________________ Phone: ______________

Additional services desired: ______________________________________

____

To protect your horse business, it is imperative that all riders who patronize your barn sign a liability release form. Liability laws, however, vary from state to state. Consult with an attorney in your area who is familiar with equine business issues and who can provide you with the liability forms you'll need.

(continued)

Health Record

Vaccinations	Date	Deworming	Date

Shoeing Record

Farrier	Service	Amount Paid	Date

Board/Services Payment Record

Date	Charges	Payments

APPENDIX B

Shoeing Record

Codes: T = trim, R = reset, N = new, S = special, P = pads, F = front only

Name of Horse	Jan	Feb	Mar	Apr	May	Jun	Jul	Aug	Sep	Oct	Nov	Dec
1.												
2.												
3.												
4.												
5.												
6.												
7.												
8.												
9.												
10.												
11.												
12.												

APPENDIX C

Equine Lease Agreement

This agreement entered into on the _______ day of ___________________, ________, (date) between ____________________________________ (the Owner) of ________________, ________, (city, state) and _____________________________________ (Lessee) of ____________, ________, (city, state).

WITNESSETH: Owner does hereby lease to Lessee and Lessee does hereby lease from the Owner the _____________________________ (color) _____________________ (sex) known as ____ (horse's name). The lease shall be for a period of ___________ months, beginning the _______ day of ______________________, _______. (date)

In exchange for the exclusive use of the above-named ____________________ (mare, gelding, or stallion) _________________________________ (horse's name) during the period of this lease, the Lessee does hereby agree to assume all responsibilities and to pay all normal and necessary expenses for the care of said horse consistent with the practices of good animal husbandry including, but not limited to, board, worming, veterinary expenses, shoeing, trimming, and hauling.

Lessee warrants that he/she has inspected said horse and agrees to accept said horse in present condition. Lessee shall pay and provide for the transportation of the horse from the Lessee to the Owner at the termination of the lease.

Owner shall have the right at any time, in person or by authorized agent, to go onto the Lessee's premises to inspect the horse and determine whether said horse is being properly cared for and in good health. The title and ownership of the leased horse shall be and remain in the name of the Owner. Lessee shall not sell, mortgage, or encumber this leased horse in any manner whatsoever. Lessee shall not assign this lease nor sublease the horse covered hereby.

If the leased horse should at any time become missing, lost, seriously injured, sick, or dead, the Lessee shall immediately notify Owner by telephone and subsequently by mail.

Owner shall not hold Lessee liable for any serious injury or death of the horse arising from events not resulting from negligence on the part of the Lessee or the Lessee's agents. Lessee shall hold the Owner harmless for any injury to persons or damages to any property caused by the leased horse.

No modification of this lease shall be binding unless in writing and executed by the parties hereto.

The undersigned Owner and Lessee accept the terms and conditions of this lease and acknowledge a copy thereof.

Owner____ Date ________

Lessee____ Date ________

APPENDIX D

Student Record

Name: ______________________________ Date of birth: __________

Address: ____

Phone: (h) ______________ (w) ______________ (c) ______________

Parents' names: ____

Contact in case of emergency: ____________________ Phone: ____________

Doctor: ______________________________ Phone: ____________

Hospital: ____

Allergies: ____

Level of riding experience: (Please circle)

Beginner Intermediate Advanced Showing

Number of years riding: __________

Date of session desired: __________

Special instructions: ______________________________________

____

____

____

Cost: __________ Paid: __________

To protect your horse business, it is imperative that all riders who patronize your barn sign a liability release form. Liability laws, however, vary from state to state. Consult with an attorney in your area who is familiar with equine business issues and who can provide you with the liability forms you'll need.

APPENDIX E

Camp Form — Sample camp application

Name of camper: ______________________________ Date of birth: __________

Address: ____

City: ____________________________ State: ______ Zip: __________

Father's name: ____

Phone: (h) ________________ (w) ________________ (c) ________________

Mother's name: ____

Phone: (h) ________________ (w) ________________ (c) ________________

Contact in case of emergency: ________________________________

Phone: (h) ________________ (w) ________________ (c) ________________

Medical concerns: ____

Allergies: ____

All campers must have their own grooming kit, including a curry comb, mane comb, hoof pick, body brush, dandy brush, and lead rope. If camper doesn't own a kit, it can be purchased for $ __________ .

Would you like to reserve one? Yes No

Our strong emphasis on safety requires all students to wear boots and ASTM-approved helmets. The helmets are $ __________ and the rubber riding boots are $ __________ .

Would you like to reserve a helmet? Yes No Size: _______

Would you like to reserve a pair of boots? Yes No Size: _______

Camp dates desired: ________________

APPENDIX F

Horsemanship Certificate

This Certificate is Awarded to

____

for Successful Completion of
The Horsemanship Program

Instructor ____________________________

Date __________

APPENDIX G

DVD Order Form

Rider's name: ______________________ Horse's name: ____________________

Address: ____

Phone: (h) ______________ (w) ______________ (c) ______________

Mailing address, if different from above: ______________________________

____

Number of copies desired: __________

Horse show, clinic, or lesson: ________

Division(s): ______________ Date: ______ Entry #: ______

Classes: ____

Ring #: ______

Special instructions: ____

____

Signature: ________________________________ Date: __________

APPENDIX H

Vehicle Maintenance Record

Vehicle ______________________ Model ______________ Year __________

Type of Work	By Whom	Date	Cost
Oil change/lube			
Oil change/lube			
Oil change/lube			
Oil change/lube			
Oil change/lube			
Oil change/lube			
Oil change/lube			
Oil change/lube			
Oil change/lube			
Oil change/lube			
Oil change/lube			
Oil change/lube			
Oil change/lube			
Oil change/lube			
Repairs			
Repairs			
Repairs			
Repairs			
Repairs			
Repairs			
Repairs			
Repairs			
Repairs			
Repairs			
Repairs			
Repairs			
Repairs			
Repairs			

APPENDIX I
Maximizing Consignment Sales

Dear Consignor,

Enclosed please find a CONSIGNOR'S CHECKLIST for your convenience. This is designed to help you prepare for the Midwestern Quarter Horse Sale. We hope this will help you get the highest possible price for your horse. Many people spend a great deal of time preparing a horse to show for ribbons and points. This auction is probably the most important "show" your horse will attend. It will have hundreds of judges, and the prize will be a check for the value of your horse. It is, therefore, in your best interest to spend time getting your horse well turned out for this sale. If you don't have very much experience selling horses at auction, please take some time to look at the checklist enclosed. If you have any questions or require any assistance, please feel free to contact Auction Services, Inc. We are eager to help you.

Sincerely,
Auction Services, Inc.

Consignor's Equipment Checklist

- ❑ Feed and hay
- ❑ Buckets
- ❑ Grooming equipment
- ❑ Halters
- ❑ A quality halter for showing your horse
- ❑ A stable halter to leave on your horse for the buyer
- ❑ Equipment to clean your stall and stable area
- ❑ Saddle and bridle if your horse is broken
- ❑ Tools to hang buckets and stall decorations

Health Requirements

	Required	Recommended
Original Coggins Report (within 12 months)	☑	❑
Interstate Health Certificate (if out of state)	☑	❑
Soundness Certificate	❑	☑
Broodmares Pregnancy Exam (within 10 days)	☑	❑
Health Records	❑	☑

Paperwork

	Required	Recommended
Registration Certificate	☑	❑
Transfer Report (properly signed)	☑	❑
Registration for Unnamed Foals (applied for)	☑	❑
Breeder's Certificate (mares that have been bred)	☑	❑

If a stallion owner withholds the Breeder's Certificate until a foal is born, a letter to this effect, signed by the stallion owner, and a copy of the signed contract must accompany the mare. This will be announced when the horse is sold.

(continued)

Preparing Your Horse for Sale

- ❑ Is your horse carrying good weight? (Flesh covers ribs, etc.) *The old horse trader says, "Fat is the best color when you want to sell a horse."*
- ❑ Is the hair coat in good condition? (clean and shiny)
- ❑ Is your horse properly clipped? (i.e., muzzle, ears, legs, feet, and bridle path)
- ❑ Does your horse load and haul well? If your horse has not loaded or trailered, practice before the sale. Plan plenty of travel time to avoid rushing and causing injury on the way to the sale.
- ❑ Are your horse's feet in good condition? (Shod or trimmed. Have this done one to three weeks before the sale. Last-minute hoof work may cause lameness without time to correct it.)
- ❑ Plan to arrive early so that you and your horse are fresh on sale day.

Salesmanship

- ❑ Bring a saddle and bridle. Show your horse in the performance demonstration. Seeing is believing. (See the attached information on the performance demonstration.)
- ❑ Stay by your stall to talk to any potential customers.
- ❑ Keep your stall area neat.
- ❑ Be pleasant and helpful.
- ❑ Stall displays and decorations will draw attention to your horse. (Include signs, pictures, trophies, ribbons, scrapbooks, and other information on your farm, including stallion service and other horses you may have for sale.)
- ❑ Show your horse in a clean halter, saddle, and bridle.

Stall Location

- ❑ Lot numbers will be posted on each stall. Make sure the correct horse is put in each stall. *Do not move your horse.*
- ❑ All of your horses will be stalled together.
- ❑ If you wish to be stalled with another consignor, contact our office no later than the Monday preceding the sale.

Some Tips on Pricing on Sale Day

1. When you bring your horse to the sale ring, let one of our handlers take it in. A member of our staff will approach you and discuss your minimum or reserve, if you have one, and relay that information to the auctioneer. He will also keep you abreast of events in the sale ring. If you decide not to sell your horse for the amount bid, tell us before the horse leaves the ring. We will announce *no sale.*

2. *Don't price your horse before the sale.* It is best to tell potential customers that you want to see what the horse brings in the sale ring. If someone is pushing you to price your horse before the sale, ask him to make an offer. This usually separates the buyers from the lookers.

3. Think carefully about the amount you will accept for your horse. Be realistic and keep an open mind. The best way to determine the value of a horse is to see what it brings in the sale ring.

4. Have a winning attitude. Be positive. You are trying to sell your horse. A potential buyer can sense whether you don't like your horse and will figure that he won't either. *We want you to get the highest possible price for your horse!*

(continued)

The Performance Demonstration

The performance demonstration is an invaluable tool for selling your horse. If your horse is broken, it will pay to show that in the demonstration.

Helpful Hints:

1. Bring a saddle and bridle that fit the horse.
2. Treat the performance demonstration like a real horse show. Wear proper attire, clean your tack, and make sure your horse is well turned out (mane pulled evenly and braided, if appropriate).
3. Do not use training gear unless it is necessary.
4. Be ready to show early on sale day.
5. *If you do not have anyone to ride your horse, please contact us. We may be able to find a rider for you.*

The demonstration will simulate horse-show conditions. Each horse will be introduced individually.

The following classes will be available:

CLASS 1

Western Pleasure — horses will be shown on the rail at a walk, jog, and lope in both directions.

CLASS 2

Hunter Under Saddle/Over Fences — horses will be shown on the rail at a walk, trot, and canter in both directions. A course will be set. If your horse jumps, you may move to the center of the area and work over fences after the flat work is completed.

CLASS 3

Green Broken Horses — shown on the rail at a walk and jog or trot. As your horse is introduced, you may move to the center to jog or lope a circle. Once your horse has been introduced, please move back to the rail.

CLASS 4

Reining and other horses will work individually. All horses to show will enter the ring and wait to be introduced. When introduced, proceed to the center of the ring as instructed. You will be given a couple of minutes to work. (If there is enough room, two horses will work at once, each taking half the ring.) *We will repeat the classes to ensure that every horse is given an opportunity to be shown.*

APPENDIX J
Organizational Calendar

Winter	Spring
• Yearly budget and goal planning	• Deworm
• Vehicle maintenance	• Take soil samples
• Organize office; update computer records and filing system	• Fertilize, use herbicide
• Send holiday newsletter	• Spring-break camp
• Have promotional event: tack cleaning or holiday party	• Advertise summer camps, send applications, hire counselors
• Conduct short course or seminar	• Farm tour; career day
• Do yearly inventory of supplies	• Clinic
• Holiday-break camp	• Lease and sell green horses — advertise
• Print applications for camp brochures, prize lists, etc.	• Mail horse-show prize lists (see horse-show calendar)
• Stationery, business cards, office supplies: update and reorder	• Advertise blanket cleaning and repair
• Train green horses; prepare for spring sale and schooling shows	• Clean and store stable blankets
• Advertise stallion service, holiday tack, and horse sales	• Organize jump party
• Vet care — vaccinate, blood tests, teeth check, etc.	• Taxes
• Restock first-aid kit	• Facility maintenance: repair, replace, and oil gates; paint, etc.
• Fire-safety drill; check/recharge fire extinguisher, smoke detectors	• Spring schooling show
• Take a vacation!	• Advertise manure sale
• Buy/maintain computer, answering machine, and drink machine	• Plant garden
• Update scrapbook/photo album	• Schedule photograph day
• Build cross-country course	• Evaluate school horse string, buy, sell, “tune up”
	• Breed stallions and mares; cull, buy, train

(continued)

APPENDIX J *(Organizational Calendar), continued*

Summer	Fall
• Summer day camps	• Fall lessons
• Horse shows — home and away (send press releases)	• Mock foxhunt (invite press)
• Clip, drag, and rotate pastures	• Deworm
• Practice fly control	• Strip stalls, lime, rebed
• Advertise for mane pulling, clipping, braiding, etc.	• Check insulation, cover windows, pipes, etc.
• Have square dance, bonfire, ice-cream social, etc.	• Vehicle maintenance — check antifreeze
• Vehicle maintenance — check coolant	• Advertise hunter clips
• Evening and weekend lessons	• Send applications for winter session and seminars; advertise
• Send applications for fall lesson sessions	• Reevaluate insurance needs and costs
• Order hay	
• Order bedding	
• Take a computer class	

APPENDIX K

Money Management Records

Note: Percentages have been rounded off to the nearest hundredth of a percent.

SAMPLE ANNUAL INCOME STATEMENT

Revenue	Amount	Percent of Total
Boarding rents	$105,000	19.46%
Horse sales	$50,000	9.27%
Commissions	$15,000	2.78%
Camps	$45,000	8.34%
Lessons	$200,000	37.07%
Special clinics	$2,000	0.37%
Horse training	$10,000	1.85%
Horse leases — long term	$20,000	3.71%
Horse rentals — short term	$25,000	4.63%
Breeding/stud fees	$25,000	4.63%
Horse-show fees	$15,000	2.78%
Judging fees	$1,000	0.19%
Tack sales	$15,000	2.78%
Book/video sales	$3,000	0.56%
Concessions (drinks)	$1,500	0.28%
Grooming (braiding, clipping)	$3,000	0.56%
Manure sales	$2,000	0.37%
Trailering	$2,000	0.37%
Total Revenue	**$539,500**	**100.00%**

Operating Expenses	Amount	Percent of Total Revenue
Cost of goods sold		
* Horses	$35,000	6.49%
* Tack	$5,000	0.93%
* Books/videos	$500	0.09%
* Concessions	$500	0.09%
* Horse show (ribbons, etc.)	$4,000	0.74%
Salaries	$100,000	18.54%
Other payroll (SS tax, insurance, etc.)	$20,000	3.71%
Feed		
* Hay	$12,500	2.32%
* Grain	$20,000	3.71%
Veterinarian (fees, medicine)	$3,000	0.56%

(continued)

APPENDIX K *(Money Management Records), continued*

Operating Expenses (continued)	Amount	Percent of Total Revenue
Bedding	$3,000	0.56%
Supplies		
office	$1,000	0.19%
barn	$500	0.09%
other	$500	0.09%
Advertising	$3,000	0.56%
Postage	$600	0.11%
Fuel	$3,500	0.65%
Utilities	$7,000	1.30%
Vehicle repair	$3,000	0.56%
Farrier	$4,000	0.74%
Other	$1,000	0.19%
Total Operating Costs	**$227,600**	**42.19%**
Gross Operating Profit	**$311,900**	**57.81%**

Fixed Overhead		
Rent	$0	0.00%
Interest expense	$40,000	7.41%
Insurance	$10,000	1.85%
Depreciation	$40,000	7.41%
Other	$0	0.00%
Total Fixed Costs	**$90,000**	**16.67%**
Pretax Profit	**$221,900**	**41.13%**
Income Tax	**$73,227**	**13.57%**
Net Income	**$148,673**	**27.56%**

CASH-FLOW STATEMENT

Category	Amount	Increase (+) or Decrease (-) in Cash
Net income	$148,673	+
Depreciation	$40,000	+
Capital expenditures	($20,000)	-
Debt servicing: principal	($16,000)	-
Changes in working capital		
* increase in receivables	$0	-
* decrease in receivables	$0	+
* increase in payables	$0	+
* decrease in payables	$0	-
* increase in inventories	$0	-
* decrease in inventories	$0	+
Total Cash Flow	**$152,673**	**28.30%**

INCOME STATEMENT

Revenue	Amount	Percent of Total Revenue
Boarding rents		
Horse sales		
Commissions		
Camps		
Lessons		
Special clinics		
Horse training		
Horse leases — long term		
Horse rentals — short term		
Breeding/stud fees		
Horse show fees		
Judging fees		
Tack sales		
Book/video sales		
Concessions (drinks)		
Grooming (braiding, clipping)		
Manure sales		
Trailering		
Total Revenue		

(continued)

APPENDIX K *(Money Management Records), continued*

Operating Expenses	Amount	Percent of Total Revenue
Cost of goods sold		
* Horses	______	______
* Tack	______	______
* Books/videos	______	______
* Concessions	______	______
* Horse show (ribbons, etc.)	______	______
Salaries	______	______
Other payroll (SS tax, insurance, etc.)	______	______
Feed		
* Hay	______	______
* Grain	______	______
Veterinarian (fees, medicine)	______	______
Bedding	______	______
Supplies	______	______
* office	______	______
* barn	______	______
* other	______	______
Advertising	______	______
Postage	______	______
Fuel	______	______
Utilities	______	______
Vehicle repair	______	______
Farrier	______	______
Other	______	______
Total Operating Costs	______	______
Gross Operating Profit	______	______

Fixed Overhead		
Rent	______	______
Interest expense	______	______
Insurance	______	______
Depreciation	______	______
Other	______	______
Total Fixed Costs	______	______
Pre-Tax Profit	______	______
Income tax	______	______
Net Income	______	______

CASH-FLOW STATEMENT

Category	Amount	Increase (+) or Decrease (-) in Cash
Net income	______	+
Depreciation	______	+
Capital expenditures	______	-
Debt servicing: principal	______	-
Changes in working capital		
* increase in receivables	______	-
* decrease in receivables	______	+
* increase in payables	______	+
* decrease in payables	______	-
* increase in inventories	______	-
* decrease in inventories	______	+
Total Cash Flow	______	______

(continued)

APPENDIX K *(Money Management Records), continued*

PARTIAL BUDGET

Change being considered: ______________________________

(1) ADDED RECEIPTS

______________________________ $ __________

______________________________ $ __________

______________________________ $ __________

______________________________ $ __________

______________________________ $ __________

______________________________ $ __________

$ __________

(2) REDUCED COSTS

______________________________ $ __________

______________________________ $ __________

______________________________ $ __________

______________________________ $ __________

______________________________ $ __________

______________________________ $ __________

$ __________

(A) ADDED RECEIPTS + REDUCED COSTS $ __________

(3) REDUCED RECEIPTS

______________________________ $ __________

______________________________ $ __________

______________________________ $ __________

______________________________ $ __________

______________________________ $ __________

______________________________ $ __________

$ __________

(4) ADDED COSTS

______________________________ $ __________

______________________________ $ __________

______________________________ $ __________

______________________________ $ __________

______________________________ $ __________

______________________________ $ __________

$ __________

(B) REDUCED RECEIPTS + ADDED COSTS $ __________

(C) NET DIFFERENCE DUE TO CHANGE (LINE A – LINE B) $ __________

APPENDIX L

Web Sites

The following sites are referred to in the text and / or are helpful national organizations.

UMBRELLA ORGANIZATIONS

American Horse Council
www.horsecouncil.org
202-296-4031

United States Equestrian Federation
www.usef.org
859-258-2472

RIDING PROGRAMS

American Quarter Horse Association
www.aqha.com
806-376-4811

Virginia Quarter Horse Riding Program
www.vaquarterhorse.com

J.A. Allen and Co. (international programs); London, England
www.halebooks.com
+44(0)1892 837171

DRIVING ASSOCIATIONS

Rural Heritage
www.ruralheritage.com

Carriage Operators of North America (CONA)
www.cona.org
651-303-4157

THERAPEUTIC RIDING

Cheff Center
www.cheffcenter.org
269-731-4471

NARHA (North American Riding for the Handicapped Association)
www.narha.org
800-369-7433 or 303-452-1212

MEDICAL AND RESCUE ORGANIZATIONS

American Veterinary Medical Association
800-248-2862
www.avma.org

Association of American Horse Practitioners
859-233-0147
www.aaep.org

Unwanted Horse Coalition
202-296-4031
www.unwantedhorsecoalition.org

BUYING AND SELLING HORSES ONLINE

Dream Horse Classifieds
www.dreamhorse.com

Equine.com
www.equine.com

EquineHits.ocm
www.equinehits.com

HorseTopia.com
www.horsetopia.com

USEFUL BUSINESS SERVICES

Markel Horse Insurance
www.horseinsurance.com
800-842-5017

Online Printing Service
www.vistaprint.com

INDEX

Numbers appearing in *italics* indicate that an illustration appears on that page.

D

E

F

G

H

I

R

T

U

W

Other Storey Titles You Will Enjoy

The Foaling Primer, by Cynthia McFarland.
A chronicle of the first year of a horse's life in amazing, up-close photographs and detailed descriptions.
160 pages. Paper. ISBN 978-1-58017-608-8.

Games on Horseback, by Betty Bennett-Talbot and Steven Bennett.
A great collection of more than 50 safe, exciting, and challenging games for horse and rider.
144 pages. Paper. ISBN 978-1-58017-134-2.

The Green Guide for Horse Owners and Riders, by Heather Cook.
A thorough guide to green horse-care alternatives, from environmentally sensitive trail riding to building green barns.
240 pages. Paper. ISBN 978-1-60342-147-8.

Horsekeeping on a Small Acreage, by Cherry Hill.
A thoroughly updated, full-color edition of the author's best-selling classic about how to have efficient operations and happy horses.
320 pages. Paper. ISBN 978-1-58017-535-7.

Judy Richter's Riding for Kids. A comprehensive handbook to teach young riders the essentials of horsemanship.
144 pages. Paper. ISBN 978-1-58017-510-4.

Teaching Safe Horsemanship, by Jan Dawson.
A comprehensive handbook that teaches both English and Western riding instructors how to create a safe riding environment.
160 pages. Paper. ISBN 978-1-58017-515-9.

These and other books from Storey Publishing are available wherever quality books are sold or by calling 1-800-441-5700.
Visit us at *www.storey.com.*